HOW TO MEET AND TALK TO Anyone ... Anywhere ... Anytime

Simple Strategies for Great Conversations

Marvin Brown

HOW TO MEET AND TALK TO Anyone ... Anywhere ... Anytime

Simple Strategies for Great Conversations

Marvin Brown

Contact Strategies LLC
New York City, NY

If you learn what good meeting-someone-
for-the-first-time conversationalists do, you,
too, can become a great conversationalist.
It really is that simple.

Acknowledgments

To my friend, Nick Murray, who twice in my life gave me the gift of knowing that I had a gift.

John Sommers, as you look down, please know how your important input and confidence in me were the "wind behind my back."

My grateful thanks to my editor, Janet Spencer King. Janet's editing skills were as important to me as a director is to making a great movie. The manuscript was there, but someone had to bring it to life without interfering with the message. Janet did that for me. She captured and retained my style of writing, while at the same time, eloquently parsing my grammar.

I would like to dedicate the last words of this page to Rita Gorman, without whose loyalty and attention to detail this book might never have been completed.

Contents

Introduction

When two strangers attempt to meet, consciously or unconsciously, certain steps of engagement are always taken. Sometimes, these steps occur rather quickly and naturally. For example, two people meet, they introduce themselves, they talk, and the encounter takes off. It is done, it is proper, and it happens to all of us.

Too often, however, people have to choreograph these steps in an elaborate way. For some reason, our society and our culture do not provide us with a commonly accepted verbal expression or well-known non-verbal physical gesture that allows us to approach another human being we don't know and in effect say:

> "Hi! My name is Marvin Brown. You look like an interesting person, someone I would like to meet. Do you think it would be possible for us to stop and talk for a few minutes to see if we have something in common? Who knows, maybe we do. If so, we might want to meet again. Or, under certain circumstances, even date. Wouldn't that be great? On the other hand, if we don't have anything in common, then no hard feelings."

This kind of meeting ritual initiated by a commonly known gesture might be the logical, the sensible, and the perfect thing to do. But as we all know, that's not how the system works.

Gestures

All cultures have gestures that are commonly understood and play an important role in everyday communication. Sometimes, they are used to add emphasis to what is being said. In other cases, a gesture may actually communicate an entire message on its own without need of any words, as we see in the examples that follow:

- Shaking a fist to show anger
- Tapping two fingers on your wrist to indicate time is running short
- Clapping after a performance to express approval
- Scratching your head to show confusion
- Pretending to yawn to show disinterest or boredom
- Raising your hand to get someone's attention
- A shrug of the shoulders to indicate "I don't know" or "I don't care."
- Rubbing your stomach to express hunger

Developing the social skills to meet people easily and effortlessly opens the door to having many more friends and acquaintances and a wider array of personality types and backgrounds. The importance of having these skills cannot be overstated.

If you lack the skills to meet the people you want to meet, when you want to meet them, you are abdicating an important personal freedom in your life— that of selecting to meet people you find attractive, interesting, or just plain nice.

Let's say you go to a party alone or you join a gym for the first time. In either environment, there may be fifty-or-so people you don't know. In other words, they are strangers to you— just as you are a stranger to them. Almost none of those people will make an effort to meet you or even have a brief conversation in passing.

The reason? Like the vast majority of people, they won't because they don't know how. Conversely, I'm sure you know people who always seem to be comfortable talking with just about everyone they come across, including strangers.

Meeting people doesn't scare them because they have mastered the technique of making conversation with anyone, anywhere. All you have to do is learn what these people already know. It really is that simple.

Once you know how to start a conversation, you will no longer have to limit yourself to meeting only people who have chosen to meet you. If you are single, the person you decide to introduce yourself to might someday become your mate. Or the outcome may be less dramatic, but important to you at the time, such as chatting with someone in an airport lounge while you wait for a long delayed flight.

Your new skills will help you interact with people at work, where meeting the right person could further your career, or simply make the daily experience more pleasant, friendlier, and yes, serene. Then of course, there are the many times during the course of daily life as you wander about the town or city you live in when you are physically close enough to people you don't know to engage them in pleasantries—if you know how. Being able to greet, meet, and get to know enough people can make even big cities feel like a small town.

Programmed to a Cultural System

We are all programmed to the cultural system we live in. Even when we don't feel like it, we are expected to be polite, to say "hello," "goodbye," "excuse me," and "thank you." We are taught to shake hands, wear proper attire, be clean, show good manners, and not stare at strangers. These are the more obvious and superficial rules of our society. I mention them only to make you aware that there is a system.

I have studied our cultural system extensively over the years and have come to recognize that what most people assume to be nothing but unimportant social trivia in fact has great significance. In this book, I explain why certain often overlooked interpersonal communication techniques are crucial to the skills of meeting people in a comfortable, easy way.

Developing the skills to meet people confidently and successfully is a lifetime gift that you can give to yourself. This book will teach you how. In it you will learn how to start a conversation, have a conversation, and, yes, end a conversation in a way that is comfortable for you and for the person you just met.

"What do I talk about?" is a problem you will never ever face again whether at business or social gatherings, or in any of the one-on-one encounters that crop up almost daily in life. This book is a must-read for everyone who wants to learn the skills necessary to become a superior conversationalist. Take control of your life. Learn how to meet anyone . . . anywhere . . . anytime.

Chapter 1

The Beginning

Meeting-people-for-the-first-time conversational skills are perhaps the most neglected social skills in our society. It's a national affliction. If this were a disease, we would call it an epidemic.

Skills that will allow you to meet and have a conversation with anyone, anywhere, anytime in America can be learned. All you have to do is learn what good "meeting-someone-for-the-first-time" conversationalists do. It's like magic. If you learn what a magician does, you, too, can be a magician.

It is the same with becoming a good conversationalist. Instead of dazzling people by making an elephant appear and disappear, you can transform yourself into a person who can:

• Start conversations with people you would like to meet at a party, a museum, the beach, the workplace, while on vacation, the gym, during business conferences, in your neighborhood, in other words, anyone . . . anywhere . . . anytime.

• Unlock the mystery of small talk, so you can freely engage people in all kinds of social and business settings, using everyday, simple English that works.

• Bounce from "small talk" to "interesting conversational talk" with whom you want, whenever you want, wherever you want.

• Enter a crowded room of strangers at a party or business conference and easily and comfortably join any group.

• Make a great first and lasting impression.

• Change topics that bore you without insulting your conversational partner.

• Never be at a loss for words or subjects to talk about.

• Talk comfortably with authority figures.

• Disengage from conversations as easily and as gracefully as you started them.

• Discover the hidden power of eye contact.

• Easily avoid those dreaded moments of conversational silence with anyone at anytime.

• Use body language or "nonverbal communication" to communicate silently and elegantly—for example, learn why a smile is the clearest, least confusing, and most universally used communication signal in the world.

These are skills that will not only change your life, they will also last a lifetime.

Stranger Anxiety

While the greatest social fear in America is the fear of public speaking, not far behind is speaking to strangers. An astonishing 90 percent of the population experiences uncomfortable feelings of shyness when trying to start and have a conversation with a stranger. We're not talking about conversations with friends, family members, co-workers, or acquaintances, but rather with people they don't know—strangers.

Let me explain more fully what I mean when I use the word "stranger." Let's assume you are in a safe environment and look at it from the point of view of the strangers around you. To them, you are the stranger and consequently, you are someone most people are nervous to approach to start a conversation.

Think about that. How many people who are strangers regularly stop you to start a conversation? Very few I'm sure. It's not that people are afraid of physical harm or of saying something offensive. Rather, they often feel they won't say something interesting enough, sophisticated enough, witty enough, or charming enough. Simply put, they just don't think they know the right thing to say. Feelings of anxiety engulf them and that prevents them from approaching people they don't know.

Anxiety is a feeling of apprehension or nervousness about an upcoming event that a person feels may not go well and is unsure about how to handle. Not all anxiety is bad. When we are preparing for an exam, a public speaking event, climbing a mountain, running a marathon, or going on stage, anxiety is nature's way of priming us to rise to the occasion.

But meeting people for the first time creates anxiety for millions of people because they fear the experience won't go well and they don't know how to make it better.

Logically, this lack of knowledge of what to say translates into a lack of confidence, which then leads to feelings of shyness. If this is what happens to you, don't make the mistake of believing your discomfort is rooted in an inbred shyness. Believing that would take a lot of time and energy to change this aspect of your life. Instead, for now, accept that the reason you are uncomfortable is simply a lack of knowledge. It has been proven time and time again that once people know what to say, their feelings of shyness mysteriously fade away.

In this book you will learn what to say and what to do to make the anxiety of introducing yourself to anyone, anywhere, anytime dwindle away or totally disappear. For example: This book will present to you ten magic words that will never leave you at a loss for something to say, whenever you want to meet and have a conversation with anyone, anywhere, anytime.

The reality of shyness. It doesn't necessarily mean you are a shy person just because you sometimes feel overwhelmed by shyness when thinking about approaching a stranger. Behavior that comes spontaneously for some people often does not come easily for others. I'm sure you know people who are so easy in conversation they seem to have what we call a "gift of gab." But it's not really a gift.

Nobody bought them a gift of gab as a birthday present. Feeling shy about starting a conversation with a stranger doesn't necessarily indicate a personality trait. In fact it's no different than getting angry about how someone gave you bad service or pushed ahead of you in line. Occasionally losing your temper doesn't mean you're an angry person. Similarly, it doesn't necessarily mean you're a shy person because you haven't yet learned how to meet people you haven't met before.

If you have a problem meeting and talking to strangers, it's not that you can't. **Shyness about meeting people is not destiny.** It's just that you haven't yet learned how to develop your underlying ability to turn it into a skill. That is how we learn to play golf, tennis, ski, ballroom dance—or become a good "meeting-someone-for-the-first-time" conversationalist. As with all skills, you develop it by emulating others, working with a coach, and patience and practice.

Now you are working to master the social skills you need to meet anyone, anywhere, anytime. This book will be your guide, and I will be your coach. All the communication tools and conversational techniques I present are concise, practical, immediately usable, and are the ones that great conversationalists use in their everyday life.

**All of us can be better tomorrow than we are today,
if we do something different today than what
we did yesterday.**

Let's get started.

Chapter 2

The Anatomy of Starting
a Conversation

For most people, the biggest barrier to initiating a conversation with someone they don't know is—literally—not knowing how to start. Let's find a solution to this problem. If a car, computer, TV, or any other item breaks, you need to know how it works before you can try to fix it. What are its parts? Break it down. In that same way, we will now break down all the parts necessary to start a conversation with a stranger.

The only way you can start a conversation with any-one—someone you know or someone you are meeting for the first time—is with a question, a declarative statement, or a combination of a question and a declarative statement.

• **A question:** We all develop different levels of knowledge. Some of you know things about science, computers, music, art, literature, or cooking that I will never know. However, there are many common things we all know. If someone asks us, any of us, a question, we know what to do. We answer the question even if to say, "I don't know the answer to that question."

• **A declarative statement:** Unlike a question, a declarative statement is something you declare, something you state. In the simplest terms, a declarative statement is anything you say that isn't a question.

And as amazing as it may seem, that's it. I say amazing because a lot of people think the art of speaking to complete strangers is complicated or mysterious. It may still seem complicated to you because we haven't gotten into the material yet, but at least it should no longer be a mystery.

You can start a conversation with someone you know or someone you're meeting for the first time only with a question, a declarative statement, or a combination of a question and a declarative statement. That's it. End of mystery.

So here we are—declarative statements or questions. I use them to start hundreds of conversations a year, many in elevators when only one other person is present. In the winter, I might say:

"Boy, it sure is cold today." (declarative statement)

"What a great day it is today. The weather is perfect, isn't it?" (declarative statement followed by a question)

7

On a Monday:

"Well, here we are again. Isn't it amazing how fast the weekend goes?" (declarative statement followed by a question)

If it's been raining for two days, I might say:

"Did you hear the weather forecast? Is it going to rain again tomorrow?"

(two questions)

I have used all of these openings when starting conversations with total strangers, and have never had an embarrassing moment as a result.

Now remember, we are in an elevator. This is not going to be an intense conversation. It's even less intense than what we call "chitchat." Let's call it "quick talk" or even "elevator talk." An exchange, however brief, might go something like this:

Me: "Boy, it sure is cold today."

She: "Yes, and I hear it's going to be even colder tomorrow."

Me: "Well, I guess that's the way it's supposed to be in the winter."

She: "Yeah."

Me: "Well, have a nice day."

She: "You, too."

By this time, the elevator has usually reached my floor.

I work on the twentieth floor of a thirty-five-story office building in New York City. Because there are no other tall office buildings around us, people on the upper floors have a magnificent, unobstructed view. On numerous occasions, I've entered an elevator with one other person who pushed the button for the thirty-second floor and said:

Me: "How's the view of the city up there on the thirty-second floor? It must be great." (a question and a declarative statement)

She: "It's fabulous."

Me: "Which way do you face?'

She: "West."

Me: "So you can see New Jersey."

She: "Yes, especially on a clear day."

Me: "Oh, here's my floor. Goodbye."

She: "Goodbye."

And that's it, the ride is over. What did I do? I opened a conversation with a question and a declarative statement and had a brief, pleasant chat with a complete stranger.

Gender notes. As we go forward on our conversational journey, you will see that I use the pronouns "he" and she" arbitrarily and often in alternating fashion. At no time is this meant to obstruct, mar, or change the gender equality we have worked hard to establish in this country. In nearly all cases, you could easily reverse these pronouns, and in no way would that alter the importance of the examples. The changing pronouns simply reflect my desire to keep the text lively—and in a small way acknowledge the success of gender equality.

Get Started Now

So here's your homework assignment. Start having brief conversations with people you don't know in contained environments, such as in an elevator or while waiting in line in various places. These kinds of situations are great because the surroundings allow for only a short conversation and then, bang, it's over and you're out of there. As a suggestion, consider talking about a general topic, such as the weather. Everyone loves to talk about the weather.

About weather. In New York City, we have two radio stations that announce weather forecasts every ten minutes, twenty-four hours a day. One of the stations claims that more people wake up to its call numbers than any other station in the nation. Don't tell me that people aren't interested in the weather.

Working on brief exchanges like this will show quick results, and it's your first step on the road to success. From declarative statement to declarative statement, question to question, you're on your way to being a relaxed and good "meeting-people-for-the-first-time" conversationalist. Please don't dismiss this assignment because it sounds so simple and easy to do. This is a practical, important skill you're learning. As with any skill, we all have to start at the beginning and learn the basics, just as we start in the shallow end of the pool when learning to swim, the bunny slope when learning to ski, and how to hold a racket when learning tennis.

You may not work or live in a building with an elevator, but we find ourselves in contained environments all the time. For example, we while away the minutes in long lines in supermarkets, on the corner waiting for a bus, or to buy tickets to a movie. These are all good places to practice opening a brief conversation. You can also use a casual question or declarative statement while watching an event, such as a parade or a sporting match.

"What a wonderful event." (declarative statement)

"Wasn't that float gorgeous?" (question)

"We're lucky that the weather turned out so great today." (declarative statement)

No one can take short cuts when learning a skill. For our purposes, if you are thinking, "I don't want to bother with this elementary conversational stuff, so just give me some good opening lines to use on various occasions, it's like saying to a piano teacher: 'I don't want to learn how to play the scales, just teach me how to move my fingers, so I can play a Rachmaninoff piano concerto.'" It doesn't work that way. You must practice, so that it becomes a reflex action. And as we all know, this can only come about by doing it. Once you have mastered this and have learned the *ten magical words* with which to start a conversation (and which I will teach you in the next chapter), you'll be able to meet and have a conversation with anyone, anywhere, anytime.

Self-visualization. This is a mental technique that helps a lot of people reach levels of achievement they would otherwise not realize. It's a process in which you use your imagination to vividly visualize events or happenings in your mind in such a way they closely parallel an event you'll be participating in. Actors, dancers, singers, comedians, public speakers, and athletes all use self-visualization extensively to improve their ability to perform. They repeatedly visualize themselves acting out every aspect of their skill in their minds *as if it were actually happening*, seeing themselves in "real" time or in slow motion, observing their weaknesses and strengths in order to improve. Take golfers—if they want to perfect a golf stroke, they visualize the greenway, the air, the sky, and the presence of other players watching them as they play. With tennis, visualizations might include the activity and noise from others on adjacent courts as well as spectators walking around, cheering someone on, or quietly watching. In other words, when self-visualizing, it is important to take in all the distractions along with the actions. An actor must feel the power of an audience waiting to be pleased, the presence of other actors on stage, as well as those standing and observing in the wings—in short, everything that he or she will likely encounter in real life. Neurologically, the visual repetition of the activity trains the nerve cells in the brain associated with the action to perform automatically, known to most of us as a reflex action.

Self-visualization is not just for sports and entertainment. People find this technique helpful in various aspects of their everyday lives. For instance, many people work hard to get into management. Then one day, they get the new job title and find themselves facing the biggest social fear experienced in this and almost every other country in the world—public speaking.

They have to give a presentation about what's going on in their department to a group of senior vice presidents. Visiting the room where the meeting will take place and visualizing making the presentation helps to ease their tension during the presentation itself. Having been there before makes it easier to be there again.

Self-visualization is a tool that will help you become proficient in many techniques described in this book even before you test them in the world. Using it regularly will bring you a lot closer and a lot faster to your goal. At appropriate times in this book, I'll remind you of this concept.

Chapter 3

Ten Magical Words for Starting a Conversation

As this book's title makes clear, it is about meeting and having a conversation with *anyone . . . anywhere . . . anytime.* The person you approach might be a man or a woman, older or younger than you, American or not. The age, gender, and nationality are irrelevant. What is important is that if you don't take the first step in initiating a conversation, most people won't start one with you either. Think of people as being "voice activated." You get them to speak to you by first speaking to them. Most people want to be friendly; they just need help getting started.

So what do you say? How do you begin an encounter with another human being? I'm now going to give you ten magical words that will always help you decide what declarative statement to make or what question to ask to begin a conversation with a stranger. Whenever you see someone you'd like to talk to, think of these **ten magical words** and presto, you will find the appropriate words to use so the person will respond.

As promised, here they are: Use the environment around you and find an environmental prop. Let me repeat that. **Use the environment around you and find an environmental prop.**

10 magical words

By using the resources around you as a starting point, you don't have to worry about being creative or brilliant. Pay attention to your surroundings. Stay in the moment. After a while, you'll enjoy this process because it works every time. **These ten magical words are going to change your life.**

As a reminder, it will be helpful in your learning process to visualize yourself in each of the following situations. These are not reality show exercises. They are real-life experiences that happen every day all over America to people like you.

At the zoo. You are standing in front of the tiger exhibit. Next to you is someone you think you'd like to meet, or at least pass a moment with. Using the tigers as an environmental prop, you try to share the experience. Here are three examples, using plain, simple, everyday English, to start a conversation with a stranger in that situation:

- I love cats! Aren't they beautiful?
- I wonder how old they are and how long they live.
- They look so peaceful. It's hard to imagine they're man-eaters.

15

On the other hand, imagine someone next to you starting a conversation with: "You seem intrigued by this animal. This is your lucky day. I'm a zoologist and I can tell you the entire history of this animal. It's a direct descendant of a Bengalese Zaphor, a small dinosaur that lived in 3 B.C. It was an herbivorous animal that lived in the marshes . . ."

As the zoologist rambles on, you might be thinking, "Help! Get me out of here. I was minding my own business enjoying a peaceful day off at the zoo, reliving my childhood, when this intellectual bore got his claws into me."

What the zoologist doesn't realize is that he doesn't have to be brilliant to break the ice. An extensive vocabulary is valuable for reading because we accept that writers sometimes use bigger words than most of us. On the other hand, if someone you just met throws several multisyllabic postgraduate words your way, you may tag that person as pompous. Yes, your vocabulary is an important part of the way people perceive you. Just be careful not to overuse it when meeting people for the first time. When in doubt, **use the environment around you, find an environmental prop**—and use plain, simple English. Here is another example.

At a workshop/seminar. During the break, you find yourself standing next to one or more of the attendees. Using the workshop as an environmental prop, you can say:
- I thought she made an interesting point about . . .
- I'm enjoying this lecture/workshop so far. How about you?
- How long have you been interested in modern art?

Wisdom in Ten Magical Words

Showing an interest in a conversational prop is an indirect, non-threatening way of showing interest in a person. With a prop, you not only don't put your ego on the line, you also don't crowd the other person. People won't feel pressured as they might with a more direct approach. For example, you don't have to go up to someone and actually say: "You look like an interesting person and I'd like to get to know you." That would be too direct.

Instead, find a conversational prop to open the encounter. By using this technique, you can relax and you won't have to agonize over trying to say something fascinating, charming, witty, or clever. Almost any declarative statement you use, or any question you ask in plain, simple English that uses an environmental prop will work as an opener, or an icebreaker.

Other Examples

On vacation at the hotel swimming pool. You're lying on one of many beach chairs closely arranged around the hotel's swimming pool. Someone sits down in the chair next to you. You're on vacation, a time and place to be friendly, so you decide to strike up a conversation with this person. Here, the hotel or the vacation itself is the environmental prop:

- This is a great place, isn't it?
- How's your vacation going so far?
- I've never been here before. Have you?
- Where did you fly in from? (Where do you live?)

"Give a man a fish and he will eat for a day; teach him how to fish and you will feed him for life." (Anonymous)

Let's say I offered you a list of one hundred perfect opening one-liners to use when you want to meet someone. Would you really have the time and inclination to memorize them? Having a formula is much better. With a formula, all you need is a central object or theme and one other person. Forget about memorizing one-liners. This book is about teaching you how to fish.

At a museum. You have plans to see the Picasso exhibition with a friend who cancels at the last minute. You go anyway. You may have run out of friends, but you haven't run out of strangers. A common interest in the artist offers an easy link between you and other people attending the exhibit. You stop and look at a picture that catches your eye. Standing next to you is a person already engrossed in the same painting. You decide to be friendly and start a conversation. Using the picture as an environmental prop, you say:

- Aren't his colors amazing?
- Abstract art is so interesting, isn't it?
- Isn't that a great painting?

The encounter may be politely brief, or you and your new acquaintance may explore other art works together. Either way it's easy to see how you took this person out of his isolation and into your friendly world. This is a perfect example of people being voice-activated. While people may want to talk to you, they may not have the courage or the knowledge of what to say to start a conversation as you now have. Nevertheless, even if they lack that courage or knowledge, once you open up the conversation, it's my experience that most people are happy to respond.

On a corner waiting to cross the street at the light.
Walking down the street, you stop at a corner for a red light. A person with a dog on a leash walks up next to you. Using the dog as an environmental prop, you can open a brief social encounter:
  • What a beautiful dog! What's her name?
  • Oh, what a cute dog! How old is he?
  • Does he bite? Just kidding.

Pets are wonderful props for breaking the ice and provide one of the easiest, surest ways to initiate a conversation with a new person.

At the beach. You are standing ankle-deep in the water. Someone walks up and stands far enough away so as not to crowd you, but close enough to be heard. You decide you want to meet this person. Using the water, weather, locale, boats, or swimmers as an environmental prop, you can start a friendly conversation by saying:
  • Great day, isn't it?
  • The water's so calm today.
  • This sure beats the city.
  • That looks like a beautiful yacht. Maybe we can bum a ride.
  • Do you know if the water is normally this cold/warm?

Where can you meet people? Meeting people, if only casually and temporarily, does not require a cast of hundreds, or even dozens. It takes only you and one other person. By using a central object, theme, or issue as an environmental prop to start a conversation, you can meet *anyone, anywhere, anytime*.

At an office party. You just joined XYZ Corporation on December 1st. The corporation employs four hundred people. You find yourself alone at the year-end office party, which is going full blast. At the bar while waiting to be served, you turn to the person standing next to you, whom you assume works for the corporation, and say:

- Hi! My name is Jordyn. I just joined the company. I work in sales.
- I'm Ben and I work in accounting. What territory do you cover?

At a party. You fly to California to see an old friend, and while you are there, she throws a party where you know no one. You see someone at the buffet table you'd like to meet. You walk up to the person and, using the food, house, or your relationship with the host as an environmental prop, you say:

- What a great party. Have you tried the shrimp yet?
- I'm a friend of Miriam. We were neighbors when she used to live in Chicago. How about you?
- Everything on the table looks so delicious. I guess my dieting will have to wait one more day.

At a flea market, antique show, trade show, or street or craft fair. Although you find yourself alone, you now know that you don't need to stay alone. While you're looking at an exhibit, examining an artifact, standing in front of a booth, or waiting in line to buy a snack from a food vendor, someone approaches and stands two to three feet away from you. You say:

• I'm really glad I came. This is a terrific show and, as they say, "So much to see, so little time."

• I just got here a few minutes ago. Any booths or exhibits you've been to that I shouldn't miss?

On an airplane. You settle into your aisle seat and grimly prepare for a six-hour cross-country flight. Someone sits down next to you. Knowing there is no quicker way to pass the time, you decide to be friendly and start a conversation. You might say:

• What a pleasure, we left on time.

• It looks like a full flight. Every seat seems to be taken.

• Are you traveling on business or pleasure?

• Are you heading home?

Take the Challenge

Using each of the environments that follow, ask yourself what you could say to start a conversation there with someone you don't know. I have suggestions for you, but first, let me challenge you to generate your own spontaneous comments. I say spontaneous because you should never have to think of what to say. It is the commonality of the environment you share that will inspire your comments. Okay, maybe not spontaneously at first, but with a little practice, you'll see how easily your comments become spontaneous. And don't forget to visualize yourself in each environment.

- Wine-tasting event
- Ski lift line
- Line to buy tickets to an event
- Charity function
- Bookstore
- Laundry room
- Intermission at a show
- Religious services
- Child's soccer game
- Tourist attraction

Remember, you don't need to commit to a long, intellectual discourse to gain someone's attention and start a conversation. **Use the environment around you and find an environmental prop.**

- Wine-tasting event: "I always seem to like the driest of the dry. How about you?"
- Ski lift line: "It looks like this is going to be a good season for skiing, with all the snow we've had lately. Is this your first time here?"
- Line to buy tickets to an event: "This is one event I don't mind standing in line for."
- Charity function: "This is some turnout. It's nice to see so many people willing to support this cause."
- Bookstore: "I see you're looking at mystery novels. I love mysteries. Any favorites you'd recommend?"
- Laundry room: "I feel I spend my life here. It's amazing how fast laundry piles up."
- Intermission at show: "That first act was so suspenseful. I'm looking forward to seeing how this gets resolved in the second act."

- Religious services: "Isn't it great to see so many people here?"
- Child's soccer game: "That's my son, Ricky, who just kicked the ball. Is your child playing?"
- Tourist attraction: "These gardens are just beautiful. I'm glad I got here early so I can take my time walking around."

No Exceptions. We're told there is an exception to every rule. With <u>environmental props</u>, the exception to the rule is that there are no exceptions. It <u>works every time</u>. You'll never again be at a loss for words when you want to meet someone. Consider this scene: You show up at 7:00 a.m. for a doctor's appointment. Unbeknownst to you and another patient, who also had a 7:00 a.m. appointment, the doctor relocated to another office the day before. Her assistant forgot to contact either of you. The other patient and you are together looking around at an empty office. No furniture, pictures, carpeting, reception desk, or employees. What then is the environmental prop? (Consider this for a moment before reading on.)

Of course, the empty office is the prop. One of you will say something like, "Are we in the right office?"

"Is this a practical joke of some kind?"

"Time to get out the cell phone—let's call the doctor's number to see what's going on."

—using the environment

Commonality creates closeness. One of the <u>primary</u> laws of connectivity is commonality. People bond with each other more quickly when they share something in common. For example, two men, who have never met, sit next to each other on a plane. One is traveling for pleasure, the other for business. One was brought up in a small Midwestern town, the other in New York City. One is twenty-eight years old, the other sixty-eight. One is single, the other married with two children and four grandchildren. The younger man notices the older man is reading a book.

Using the title as an environmental prop, he asks:

"I couldn't help noticing you're reading a book about golf. Do you play?"

"Yes, I do. Avidly. How about you?"

"I do," the young man answers. "I live for the sport."

It's easy to imagine these two bonding. It happens all the time and, in this case, it started with a prop.

Commonality associations are just as powerful as environmental props. They create instant rapport and help keep conversations going:

- "You went to the University of Chicago. So did I."
- "You read Stephen King! I love his novels."
- "So you play chess. I love chess."
- "You were brought up in Brooklyn! So was I."
- "Your son is starting high school. My daughter just finished her first year."
- "You like to cook? I just took a class in pastry making."

Attention-getters. In order to meet people, you first have to say, "Hello!" Well, not literally. As you read this book, you will notice I have not included certain expressions of introduction: "Hi," "Hello," "Good morning," and especially

"Hello, how are you?" There's a good reason for this, These greetings can lead to a conversational dead end.

When you say: "Hi!"
Most people will reply: "Hi to you, too!"

When you say: "Hello!"
Most people will reply: "Hello!"

Do not use

When you say: "Good morning!"
Most people will reply: "Good morning!"

When you say: "How are you?"
Most people will reply: "I'm fine. And you?"

NOW WHAT! Exactly—the conversation doesn't go anywhere. You are back to square one and possibly an awkward moment.

The power of "Excuse me." Sometimes, especially in some formal settings, you may feel more comfortable employing a "conversational attention-getter." If so, keeping your voice light, rising, and friendly, say, "Excuse me." This alerts the person you are approaching that you are initiating contact.

- "Excuse me, isn't that a great-looking picture?"
- "Excuse me. I see you're looking at mystery novels. Can you recommend any authors you're fond of?"
- "Excuse me. Have you been coming to this aerobics class for a long time?"
- "Excuse me. I see your son is playing today. He's good."

25

Many people feel knowledge is power. Others say it is only the application of knowledge that is power. This book is about acquiring the knowledge to meet and have a conversation with anyone, anytime, anywhere. Get your money's worth by going out into the world and applying the knowledge.

Chapter 4

Continuing a Conversation

W hen engaged in a great conversation, we are not generally conscious of who is talking, who is listening, who is asking the questions, or who is answering them. The conversation flows effortlessly as one topic seamlessly merges into another. You have no doubt enjoyed conversations like this with friends and loved ones in the past. They are also possible with people you meet for the first time—those people we call strangers.

Structurally, a conversation is a two-way street during which people talk back and forth to each other and exchange information. It's that simple. But before we go any further, let's clarify the traffic rules that govern this two-way street. Or maybe I should say, let's drive down this two-way street together. By definition, the traffic goes both ways. This means your responsibility for the flow of conversation is about 50 percent. The person you are talking with is also aware of this and will generally make every effort to do his or her part. It gets easier when the conversation includes more than one person. For example, when you are engaged in a three-way conversation, each person's conversational responsibility is 33 percent; with four, it drops to 25 percent.

Conversations Can Carry Themselves

As you now know, people start conversations with declarative statements or questions. These openings are a means to an end, but they are not the end. The replies you receive to either a declarative statement or a question are treasure troves of conversational fillers that can be used to lengthen and enrich conversations.

For example, let's say you decide to begin a conversation with a question. As I mentioned in Chapter 2, people know what to do when asked a question—they answer it. This natural human reaction leads to the next conversational step that allows you to make a statement about the information you just received. In this way, the conversation feeds upon itself. You offer opinions, information, and ask questions; your conversational partner counters with opinions, information, and asks questions. Thus, much of the burden of maintaining the conversation is off everyone's shoulders, because the conversation is feeding on itself.

Other conversational rules:

- Conversations are *not* competitive events. There should never be a winner or a loser.
- It is *not* your responsibility to be amusing or entertaining during a conversation. If you are, great. If you say something funny, fine. But it isn't required. That's not a burden you should be carrying.
- It *is* your responsibility to be focused, interested, and to listen during the exchange. As you will see, besides the ten magical words, listening creates its own magic. (We will cover listening in Chapter 7.)

Scientists tell us that about 90 percent of a glacial iceberg is under water. My curiosity lacks the depth necessary for me to consider diving into frigid waters to verify this, but when someone I just met drops a conversational iceberg into our conversation, I'm willing to explore its depth. Although the following are dramatic examples, let's say someone casually says:

"Well, one of my seven brothers is a doctor."

I might say: "Did you say you are one of eight boys?"

Or:

If someone says: "Oh that was a long time ago when I tried out for a role in one of Steven Spielberg's movies."

I might say: "You tried out for a role in one of Steven Spielberg's movies? Please tell me more."

These exploratory trips are worth the effort. Personally, I make the effort, not just because I want someone to think I'm charming, but because I have found that many people can be interesting to be with if you help them elaborate on a thought or idea they just expressed. Okay . . . a side effect is that people I meet for the first time might think I'm charming because I show an interest in who they are and what they're saying. That interest enables people to feel good about themselves. When people feel good about themselves while conversing with you, they'll remember you as someone who they enjoyed meeting.

Looking for the opening to continue a conversation is an easy skill to learn. You don't have to spend money on lessons or exert yourself physically. Be interested in people and people will be interested in you.

Consider the following conversation between two co-workers:

Bill: "Hi, Max. How are you?"

Max: "Fine, Bill, and you?"

Bill: "Wonderful. I just got back from vacation."

Max: "Great. Did you have a good time?"

Bill: "Yes! I had a great time. So tell me, what do you think of those Mets?"

Max: "Doing better than I expected. By the way, have you seen _____(latest blockbuster movie)?"

Bill: "Yes, it was very funny."

Max: "The weather's been great lately, hasn't it? But hey, how are the kids?"

Bill: "Good. Rebecca is graduating from high school this year."

Max: "That's great. My kids are also doing fine. I've enrolled Don in karate, but I think he prefers playing in the band he and his friends started."

Bill: "Well, I hope it works out. I have to run now. Good to see you."

Max: "Same here."

Although Bill and Max have the power of speech, they either have limited interpersonal skills or they are simply more interested in themselves than in others. Go back and count how many opportunities they missed to make their encounter more interesting for each of them. Note in the following how even one probing question would have opened the dialogue.

Bill: "Hi, Max. How are you?"

Max: "Fine, Bill. And you?"

Bill: "Wonderful. I just got back from vacation."

Max: "I thought so. You look tanned and well rested. Where did you go?"

Bill: "Hawaii."

Max: "Did you have a good time?"

Bill: "Great."

Max: "I've never been to Hawaii. Tell me about the trip. What did you do there?"

Here are more "treasure trove" statements, along with appropriate conversation-continuing responses.

"Oh, I learned how to ride horses when I lived in Texas."

"When did you live in Texas?" A close-ended question, but one that can easily lead to open-ended ones. (I will cover more about questions and the value they have in being a good conversationalist in Chapter 5.)

31

"Thanks for noticing I lost weight. It's always a battle to stay in shape since I love to cook." (Here we have a "treasure trove" of three possible topics of conversation you can latch onto—dieting, fitness, or cooking.)

In the past, the following statements may have been submerged under the iceberg, hidden from your view. Now, as you can see, they're so obvious. Fill in the responses yourself.

"No, I never get to see that TV show. Wednesday evening is reserved for my acting class."

"I finally got my chance to see the real Animal Planet—in living color. Last April, I went on a safari."

"I'm an accountant for a large public accounting firm, but my real love is ballroom dancing."

Conversational skills are not formally taught in this country or any other country that I am aware of. So thinking of how to respond to the statements above may seem so obvious, why bother to take up space in the book? The fact is in real life, many people let the subjects pass. As I mentioned earlier, if you learn what a magician does, you, too, could become a magician. Much of it isn't that hard. Neither are the skills of being a great conversationalist. You just have to learn the rules and consciously apply them for a while. Then, like any skill, you'll do them instinctively and effortlessly.

The Bridging Technique

Sometimes a subject will come up that doesn't interest you. Let's say a person you know or just met asks: "Do you think _____ is doing a good job as mayor?" Or, "Did you see the debate last night?" These are not casual questions and the person is not taking a poll. It suggests your conversational partner is interested in politics and has something to say. And he doesn't want a one-word answer; he wants to dig deeper into the subject.

You may not want to go down that road. And if you don't, then don't. Some consider politics a topic you should avoid when meeting people for the first time. But some people might bring it up anyway, so be prepared. If the topic is mutually interesting, it can trigger a great conversation. However, if the subject doesn't interest you, in no way are you obliged to stay focused on it for any length of time. In this case, you need to be prepared to change the subject. *This is called a "bridging technique."* Here's how it works.

"I haven't made up my mind yet about the elections. I'm going to watch and listen with an open mind. *Oh, I just thought of something I've been meaning to ask you about . . .* "

"Yes, I think he's doing a great job as mayor. *Oh, by the way, did you notice the other day . . .* "

On the other hand, there may be times when you bring up a subject that your conversational partner seems reluctant to discuss. When that happens, you can graciously employ a bridging technique on yourself. That's what good conversationalists do. So right in the middle of the silence or feeling of discomfort coming your way, breathlessly say:

"Say, before I forget, can I ask you about . . . ?"

"You know, a thought just popped into my head about . . . "

The bridging technique is going to be useful to you in the future under many different circumstances. For example, all interactions, even riveting conversations, contain natural pauses. When one occurs, you can "bridge" by saying, "Oh, by the way . . ." Keep the bridging technique in your conversational arsenal.

Embedded in many conversations are other conversations. Let's say Jennifer asks if you saw the game last night. Again, it's obvious Jennifer doesn't want a yes or no answer, but wants to talk sports. There are other subjects like this. Pay attention and you will hear people drop hints of interesting topics you can explore. That is if you want to. Otherwise, just bridge yourself out and on to another topic.

Situational Friends and Social Acquaintances

There are many people we meet and interact with in our lives, but never get to know well. We may see co-workers daily, but try not to cross the privacy line. We often chat with the same people at the gym, but only briefly. We say "Hi" to our neighbors, but usually on the run, with no time for a serious conversation. These people are casual friends, or what some people call "situational friends" or "social acquaintances."

A situational friend or a social acquaintance is someone you connect with through a shared situation. They may be people you know from the gym, a golf or tennis club, yoga class, business conferences, or even at work. The feeling of liking the person is real. And it's obvious that the person also likes you. But the reality is that when the situation ends, often so does the friendship.

I've known Larry for five years and he fits this profile perfectly. He's someone I run into once or twice a month at a club we both go to. Not long ago, we were talking about the earthquakes and flooding rains that California endures from time to time. Larry replied that when he lived there, he got used to the occasional earthquake and anyway, living in such a beautiful state made any disadvantages not that bad. Again, for readers of this book, it might seem natural to pursue this comment. In reality, most people don't. This is the kind of information a great many people ignore during a conversation, even though it is the tip of the iceberg. "Larry, I didn't know you lived in California!"

- "Oh yes, for six years."
- "What took you there?"
- "My brother started a business and I went out to join him."
- "Where in California did you live?"
- "In Sausalito, just north of San Francisco."
- "What brought you back to New York?"

This kind of dialogue, not only keeps the conversation going, it also paves the way to a deeper and potentially more interesting relationship. The more curious you are about another person, the more personal information you share, the more interesting each of you becomes to the other.

A likeable thought. Research has shown what you probably have sensed yourself over the years. The more people tell you about themselves, the more they get to like you as a person. The more they share with you, the closer they feel to you.

Think of people as living novels. Everyone's life is filled with subplots. Most books have a readily accessible table of contents and index. In life, you have to hunt for them: first, through listening—not just hearing, but listening—and second, by asking good getting-to-know-you-better questions. (I'll cover more on the important subject of questions in Chapter 6.)

Again, show people you're interested in them. and they will usually become interested in you. Look at it another way: If you show someone you are not interested in them, why should they be interested in you?

Echoing → the power of silence

This book is all about how to meet and talk with people. However, there are times when the echoing technique—literally repeating back what the other person just said—is by far your best tool if you then follow it with silence. In fact, silence is one of the most effective conversational tools we possess and possibly the most under-used.

Echoing gives your conversational partner an opportunity to open up and express his passions or point of view on a subject without your sounding too challenging or confrontational to his circumstances or beliefs. As you'll see, sometimes the technique of repeating what a person said in the form of an innocent question and then silently waiting for an explanation is better than asking, "Why?" Asking why puts the person under pressure to come up with an answer to the question. But repeating the question in the manner I just described gives him the option to offer a yes or no answer or explanation. Either way, it's the other person's decision.

A friend just told you: *"I'm quitting my job"* or, *"I'm being sued."* To successfully accomplish and complete the echoing technique, simply repeat what was said in the form of a question *"You're quitting your job?"* or, *"You're being sued?"* Be sure to have a caring tone in your voice and a concerned look on your face and then remain silent. One other important point: Don't get upset about the two or three seconds of silence that may occur, while the person silently has thoughts rushing through his head. However deafening the silence may feel, your conversational partner will soon fill it with an outburst of words.

Other examples: (And remember to self-visualize yourself in each.)

A friend or co-worker tells you she is voting for a candidate in an upcoming city, state, or national election that shocks and even horrifies you.

"You're voting for who?"

(Pause, remain silent, and look at your conversational partner with a puzzled look.)

A friend, co-worker, relative, or neighbor tells you he doesn't like someone you both know. In the event you personally like the person and can't understand this person's point of view, say:

"You don't like _____?"

(Then remain silent and look at your conversational partner, again with a puzzled look.)

As a parent
Child: "Dad, I can't finish my homework assignment."
Dad: "You can't finish your homework assignment?"
Or:

Child: "Mom, I don't have the time to clean up my room."

Mom: "You don't have the time to clean up your room?"

(Remember to stay calm, look bewildered, and remain silent. Who knows, maybe there is a legitimate reason.)

At work

Employee: "I'm overloaded with work."

Supervisor: "You're overloaded with work?"

(Ask the question, look puzzled, and remain silent.)

In a shop

Even as a customer, silence can be powerful when negotiating a price.

Salesperson: "The price is $_____."

Customer: "Can you do better on that?"

(Pause and remain silent with a slightly painful look on your face.)

You've asked a question. The sales person owes you an answer. If he says, "I can't do any better," just repeat the last few words. "You can't do any better?" and again, remain silent. More often than not, if a price reduction is possible, you'll see how the power of silence works in your favor.

"Drawing on my finest command of the English language, I said nothing." —Robert Benchley, American Humorist

Talking with Authority Figures

As we have discussed, conversations are an exchange of information. Like cars on a two-way street, bits of information flow back and forth between the speakers. The responsibility for carrying a conversation is divided equally between the participants. But what if you're talking with an authority figure? In that case, the burden of carrying the conversation is overwhelmingly the responsibility of that person, not you. We live in a hierarchical society. It may sound undemocratic, but that's just the way it is. We have all accepted, consciously or unconsciously, wittingly or unwittingly, this social structure as our American way of life. Hierarchies abound. The corporate president has authority over all other executives. This is also true in:

- The legal system, where the judge rules the courtroom
- Schools, where principals supervise teachers and teachers supervise students
- Sports, where the coach is the team leader
- Job interviews, where potential employees defer to the employer

In all these cases, the person with less authority cedes conversational control to the person with more authority. That's because authority figures, not only have higher status, they also have more power. An assistant doesn't say to a senior corporate officer, "So Mrs. Brown, what are your plans this weekend? Tell me, what are you and Mr. Brown going to do?" At most she might say, "I hope you have a nice weekend, Mrs. Brown."

When you are with an authority figure, you have little or no responsibility for directing the conversation. Accept your role: Relax and enjoy it. Pay attention to what the authority figure is saying, so you can respond effectively. Use your verbal and nonverbal conversation enforcers. Nod. Smile. Maintain eye contact to show both strength and respect. You can be charming without being in control. Remember, too, that unless a subordinate has a pressing need to be somewhere, the authority figure is usually the one who signals the end of the conversation. (More on how to end conversations coming up in Chapter 8.)

Adults Rule. There is one time when just being an adult virtually always makes you the authority figure in a conversational relationship. Think back to conversations you've had with children—any children. Who controlled what you talked about? Who led the conversation? It was of course you. Children quickly learn to accept a subordinate role in face-to-face communication with adults, our first authority figures.

Opinion vs. Fact or No One Likes a Know-It-All

To protect yourself from a know-it-all label, avoid offering an opinion as fact. We are all entitled to our opinion, but a person can easily sound overbearing by offering one as fact. Preface your opinions with "It seems to me," "I believe," or, "I think."

- "It seems to me _____ is the best restaurant in the city."
- "I believe _____ should win the Academy Award for best picture."
- "I think _____ is doing a good job as president."

If you leave off the qualifier in these kinds of statements, you sound as if you're making the case without consideration of the other person's opinion. Try this exercise: Go back and re-read the sentences above and then repeat them without "It seems to me," "I believe," or "I think." It's the difference between a person who thinks for himself and one who is just opinionated. Most of becoming a good meeting-some-one-for-the-first-time conversationalist is this easy—you just have to know.

More Thoughts on How to Continue a Conversation

What do you do for a living? Many people think asking others what they do for a living is trite. It may be if someone brings it up within five minutes of meeting a person. But if you're asked this question well into a conversation, it probably means your conversational partner has come to like you. An expression of interest in what you do for a living is often a signal that she wants to find out more about who you are as a person. Take it as a compliment.

At Poolside

Let's say you're on vacation and, while lounging around the hotel pool, you get into a conversation with Leslie, someone you met the previous day. Your new acquaintance casually asks, "So tell me, what kind of work do you do back home?" You say, "I'm an executive recruiter and specialize in placing executives in the advertising industry." She seems interested and asks a couple of questions to flesh out more information about your work. Then, because you are conversationally at ease, you ask what she does for a living. As each of you talks freely and easily about what you do, the exchange of information becomes the catalyst for creating rapport. It shows you have started to hit it off. But keep in mind that it was Leslie's initial question about your work that triggered the conversational flow.

Where do you live? I recently met a man from Canada named Pierre. It struck me how little I knew about Canada, even though it's our neighbor and mostly an English-speaking country. Seizing on Canada as the conversational prop, I asked Pierre how many people lived there. I was astounded to learn that Canada has a population of only thirty-five million compared to the over three hundred million in the US. After that, the questions and answers just seemed to feed on themselves, and the conversational traffic flowed effortlessly.

I pursued the subject because I was genuinely interested in learning about Canada. My conversational partner seemed equally pleased with his 50 percent contribution to our social encounter, sharing information about his country. My questions and his answers centered around an environmental prop. That's all we needed for each of us to feel we had connected and ended up having had an interesting conversation with a "stranger."

As you can see, continuing a conversation is not that difficult as long as you keep certain things in mind.

• Always show interest in the person you're speaking with and what they're saying. From the moment of birth, babies cry out for attention. Things don't change that much as people grow up. That's why this is the first item I put on the list of things to remember to do.

• Don't worry about taking on the bulk of conversational responsibility in a one-on-one conversation or in a group. We all have equal rights . . . and responsibilities. Sometimes you will talk more, sometimes less as you listen more. Just go with the flow and enjoy the ride.

• The tip of the iceberg became an expression because emotionally and intellectually most people are generally hidden beneath the surface. Asking questions and bringing those hidden conversational topics into the open is a great way to keep the conversational traffic flowing smoothly as well as getting to know your conversational partner better.

• Knowing how to recognize and avoid uncomfortable topics is a really helpful tool. The "bridge" you use to change the subject can turn what may seem like a conversational dead end into an enjoyable encounter.

• Differentiating between talking to an "authority figure" and being one yourself allows each person to feel safe and comfortable in his or her lane as the encounter takes place.

• Avoid making opinion statements sound like facts.

• Last, but not least, use the echoing technique to show interest, but still allow the other person to respond with as much or as little information as he wants.

Learning the interpersonal, face-to-face social interaction skills in this book can bring down the glass wall between you and the people you pass by every day. With a little practice, you really can *meet and have a conversation with anyone, anywhere, anytime.* Read on. More skills are awaiting you, and so is the world.

Chapter 5

I Have a Question for You!

D o you know how most people respond when asked a question by someone who is trying to start a conversation with them? That's preposterous to ask, isn't it? As preposterous as it seems, here is the answer. People will usually answer either "Yes" or "No." That's because most people begin conversations by asking close-ended questions that elicit a "Yes" or "No" answer and nothing more.

44

- "Have you been here before?" ("Yes")
- "Do you come here often?" ("Yes")
- "Do you live in this neighborhood?" ("Yes")
- "Is it a good place to eat/dance/hang out?" ("Yes")
- "Do you find this conversation interesting?" ("No")

This is typical of the way many people initiate conversations. Information is exchanged, but not much. Whether these two people just met for the first time or know each other casually, the outcome is probably not what either really wanted. Each question was structured, so that it creates a wall between them instead of a bridge. Asking a series of close-ended questions demands little from the person answering them because close-ended questions are framed to elicit yes or no answers, or at the very most a brief, "go nowhere" statement.

- "It's hot in here, isn't it?"
- "Are you hungry?"
- "Wasn't that a good movie?"

Though most people can go beyond yes or no answers, without further prompting, few will. They provide the short answer they think the other person is looking for, and nothing else. Moreover, many close-ended questions can be answered with a nod, a grunt, or an "Uh huh." What kind of conversation is that? Even if you ask a close-ended question about an interesting topic in an interested way, the answer could still be a conversation-stopper.

"Do you think the world is doing enough about climate change?" "No."

"Don't you think it's a shame that developed countries spend more on defense than in helping the poor?" "Yes."

45

After engaging someone's attention, the aim of a good conversationalist is to make it easy for the other person to respond with more than a yes or no. You can do this by asking an open-ended question.

Open-Ended Questions

Open-ended questions require a more detailed answer than simply yes or no. This makes them a good way to lubricate the conversation. In response to such a question, people need to explain, to expound, or to share their feelings, thoughts, or knowledge on a subject you're asking about. Such elaboration is an important element of a good conversation.

- "How did you get involved in such an interesting hobby?"
- "What motivated you to move to New York?"
- "That's interesting. Tell me more about . . ."
- "Why did you decide to change careers?"
- "You seem to feel strongly about that. Why do you feel that way?"
- "That's amazing. How were you able to do that?"

In truth, many people have difficulty constructing open-ended questions. If you're good at it, great. But if this skill eludes you, don't worry. You can learn it. When you find yourself asking a close-ended question and then realize you could have phrased it in an open-ended way, don't say to yourself, "I'm terrible at this and will never learn." Instead look for an open-ended follow-up question you can ask.

For example, you bump into a coworker who just returned from a vacation to Mexico.

Q. "Susan, how was your vacation?"
   (Close-ended question.)
A. "Great!"
   (Close-ended answer.)
Q. "Tell me about it. What did you see? What did you do?"
   (Open-ended questions.)

An important tip. Here is a great tool that good conversationalists use to turn potentially dead-end conversations into interesting ones. This strategy is both effective and easy to use. Given that most people have trouble asking open-ended questions, you aren't going to hear a lot of them, so it will be up to you to turn the conversation around. When people ask you a close-ended question, give them an open-ended answer. Instead of answering with one-word responses to close-ended questions, volunteer to elaborate. Open up, expound, explain, offer an opinion, or make a statement. We can do that. Elaboration is the heart and soul of a good conversation. Don't wait for struggling conversationalists to ask you open-ended questions. Express yourself and open up the dialogue. Do it, and do it in plain, simple English.

A good conversationalist might then also ask her own open-ended question on the same subject. For example:

Close-ended question: "Did you like the movie?"

Close-ended answer: "Yes."

Open-ended answer: "Yes, I loved it! It was a thought-provoking (scary, funny) movie. The special effects were fantastic. What did you think of it?" (Open-ended question.)

Thanks to you, the conversation now has life, and all because you declined to answer with a simple yes or no. Your

open-ended answer gave what we call a "conversational handle" for the other person to grab onto. Now, he can elaborate
on your response. The best conversations feed on themselves.

What's probably the most frequently asked close-ended
question during a social exchange in America, especially on
Mondays?

Tom: "How was your weekend?"

Jerry: "Great! How was yours?"

Tom: "Terrific. Have a nice day."

Jerry: "Yeah, see you later.

Instead consider the possibility of this open-ended
answer:

Tom: "How was your weekend?"

Jerry: "Wonderful. I took the kids to that new amuse-
ment park. I think I had a better time than they did. It's been
so long since I went on all those silly rides. We even had cot-
ton candy. I felt like a kid myself. Tell me about your weekend. What did you do, Tom?"

In summary, always try to ask open-ended questions
because:

• It will make it easier for your conversational partner to
respond with an open-ended answer, which will bring life and
longevity into the conversation.

• They are a great way to follow up a close-ended question and get a real conversation going.

• By being willing to elaborate, you'll help to continue
and improve the conversation and encourage others to do the
same. Start now—train yourself to avoid one-word answers to
close-ended questions.

A few words of caution about some open-ended questions. Like all things in life, sometimes we can abuse a good thing. Some open-ended questions are so general, they can be self-defeating, just empty-talk questions that require no thought to ask and thus usually receive thoughtless answers. Here are some common empty-talk questions to avoid:

Question	Answer
"What's up?"	"Nothing much."
"How's it going?"	"Okay. Not bad."
"What's new?"	"Not much."
"What have you been up to lately?"	"Same old thing."

An important tip. After you ask a question, pause in silence. Listening to the answer shows you're interested in what the other person has to say. Whether chatting with friends or new acquaintances, showing you're interested in what they're telling you strongly indicates that you're also interested in them as people. It is a bonding technique and one of the laws of connectivity. Start practicing open-ended questions today, wait for the answer, and get a conversation going.

Chapter 6

Small Talk and Ritual Questions

People often say:
"I hate small talk. It's so much work and such a waste of time. Besides, I usually can't think of anything interesting to say."

Or:

"If I can't have an interesting conversation with someone, then I'd rather not have one at all. I have no patience chatting about the weather."

Many people who want to meet others don't even try because engaging in small talk makes them feel so uncomfortable. But here is an undeniable fact: *You can't meet people unless you're willing to engage in small talk.* Small talk is the medium that human beings use to get to know each other. It is that transitional point in a conversation when you and the person you just met are searching for subjects you can both talk about comfortably, easily, and knowledgeably. You can't get to deep talk without going through small talk. So instead of viewing it as small talk, think of it as "getting to know you" or "meeting someone for the first time" talk. It is an important step in the process of meeting people.

Here's another small talk conversational truth: *The easiest way to learn how to be good at small talk is to learn not to be afraid of it.* You're the one scaring yourself. Get rid of your misconceptions about small talk, and don't make more of it than it is. Small talk is not sophisticated, chic, or clever talk. It's just common-language talk, the type we easily engage in with our friends, family members, and workmates on a daily basis. When was the last time a friend of yours came up to you and asked:

"Do you think Tolstoy's *War and Peace* would be a bestseller if it were released today instead of when it was published way back in 1869?"

Never. They ask if you've been watching the World Series, the Super Bowl, the Olympics, the elections, or whatever riveting TV show, movie, or scandal is currently capturing the attention of most Americans. In other words, small talk.

People who are uncomfortable with small talk think they have to be unfailingly clever, charming, or witty. Don't look for something that doesn't exist. Not only will you not find it, you will miss the real solution to the problem. The secret to learning how to be good at small talk with people you just met is to do what you have been doing all your life with people you already know, namely talking about everyday things in simple everyday language. Let's say I'm at a party and someone comes up to me and asks a sophisticated question on an interesting topic:

"Are you attending the symposium next week at Sotheby's, being led by Evian DeBois? He's discussing the influence that Matisse and Picasso had on each other in the early 1900s. What do you think—did Matisse have a greater influence over Picasso or the other way around?"

If someone approached me like that, I would tell the person, "Sorry, I have a very important phone call to make," and make my escape as quickly as possible. And so would most people I know.

Everyday Talk

Good conversationalists talk about plain, simple things when trying to get to know other people. And once they know them, they continue to use plain, simple, everyday English to talk about plain, simple things. Forget about being eloquent. Even a Harvard professor doesn't say, "Oh, I feel all this angst." No, he says, "I feel lousy today." A brilliant brain surgeon doesn't say to a colleague, "I have this overwhelming feeling of ebullience today." No. She says, "I'm so happy. I'm seeing this great guy and I think the relationship is going somewhere."

Linguists tell us that words reflect their meaning. This is true in all aspects of life except *small talk*. When people hear the phrase "small talk," they try to make something out of it that it isn't. It's called small talk because that's what it is—small talk. It's not called "clever talk" or "eloquent talk" or "big talk" or "designer-label talk." If you say it's a big building, I don't think of a hut; if you say it's a small car, I don't think of a limousine.

Why do so many people think that small talk is big talk, or clever talk, or important talk? I don't know, and for our purposes, it doesn't matter. I only care that you now know that small talk is everyday talk and that you can do it if you want to. You don't have to learn it—you already know how to do it. You've been doing it all your life!

A few words about chitchat. *Chitchat* is another word for small talk. It's a social transaction, a bonding mechanism. Small talk or chitchat is what human beings do. When dogs meet for the first time, they sniff each other. Big animals might circle each other. Human beings make small talk. Small talk is the "rite of passage" to deeper and more intimate talk.

Although we don't know each other, if you and I were to meet and strike up a conversation, this is the way I would talk to you, and I hope this is the way you would talk to me—in plain, simple English about plain, everyday things.

Ritual Questions

As human beings, we use small talk and ritual questions to get to know others. A lot of people shy away from ritual questions because they think they're trite, boring, or intrusive. In reality, most people feel flattered when you ask ritual questions. The message you're sending is, *"I'm interested in getting to know you better."* Good conversationalists distinguish between showing interest and being nosy.

Showing Interest	**Nosy**
Where do you work?	How much do you earn?
What kind of work do you do?	Do you like your boss?
Where do you live?	What is your mortgage?

Ritual questions are getting-to-know-you-better talk. Environmental props allow you to make contact and start a conversation. It's ritual questions that connect you to a person.

Suppose you meet someone in a bar, on a train, or at a dinner party, and open the conversation about sports or the latest scandal: "Oh, did you catch the game? What an upset!" Or, referring to a newspaper headline about the separation of two famous celebrities: "Do you think they'll get back together?"

Regardless of the subject matter or length of the conversation, if neither of you asks a ritual question, you soon go your separate ways and in no time probably forget the conversation and even the person. That's because answers to those "trite" ritual questions were missing, just as the person is now missing from your conscious mind.

But let's say you meet Paul and learn that he lives in Connecticut and works in computers for a large corporation, loves skiing, is married with two teenage daughters, and enjoys being a soccer dad on weekends—he is someone you will remember. Gail—who just moved to Los Angeles from Texas to pursue a career in sales, is learning yoga, and has a passion for sports—is someone you'll remember long after you forgot what you talked to her about. The answers to those ritual questions are what connected you to Paul and to Gail.

Remember, this book is about *how to meet and have a conversation with anyone, anywhere, anytime.* This requires learning how to begin a conversation, have a conversation, and end a conversation with someone you haven't met before. Ultimately, the goal is to meet and to get to know people. Ritual questions are an essential part of that process, no matter whom you meet or where you meet them. Even if you're married or in a relationship, you probably remember the typical questions single people ask to try to move a relationship forward.

"What's your name?"

"Where do you live?"

"Where did you grow up?"

"Do you come from a big family?"

"Where do you work?"

This is what people do. They ask ritual questions because that's the way you get to know someone. All people, from all walks of life and at all socioeconomic levels, ask ritual questions. It's how friendships begin.

"What kind of work do you do?"

Yes, work is an appropriate subject for ritual questions. Sometimes, you get lucky and meet someone who is in an interesting line of work. But interesting or not, most people spend at least one-third of their time at work. It's a legitimate subject to raise because it is such a significant part of a person's life. And remember, this is getting-to-know-you talk. How could you not talk about work? True, some people don't like to talk about their work. If you happen to run into such a person, you'll get the point and move on to another subject. (A perfect opportunity for the bridging technique I discussed in Chapter 4.) But don't shy away from broaching the work question. Most people are happy to talk about their work.

I sat next to a character actor on a plane last year. He wasn't a famous star, but one of those actors who forged a career by playing minor roles in a lot of movies. He was instantly recognizable because he looked exactly as he does on the screen. I turned to him and asked, "Aren't you the guy I've seen on TV and in the movies?" Looking uncomfortable, he kind of brushed me off. "Yeah, yeah." Then I said, "I always enjoyed seeing you in a role. Tell me, how did you get into acting? Is it as hard as I've always heard?"

Was this a sophisticated question? Hardly. Did I ask it using plain, simple English? Absolutely. Did it provoke a long conversation? Yes. Did he enjoy the conversation as much as I did? Clearly. Besides hearing firsthand about the struggles of an aspiring actor, I found out he was a down-to-earth person—no airs, no stuffiness. I think he enjoyed telling me his story as much as I liked listening to it.

You see, it is possible to meet *anyone, anywhere, anytime*. But, before I go any further, let me make an important point. It wasn't "Just me" who met this actor. If it weren't for the strategies I used in approaching him, I'd never have been able to initiate and continue such a successful conversation. Let's go back to the beginning and review how the encounter began. His acting career was the environmental prop I used to begin the conversation. Structurally what happened wasn't any different than asking someone:

- "Isn't that a great painting?" (at a museum)
- "I'm enjoying this lecture/workshop so far. How about you?" (at a workshop or seminar)
- "This is a great place, isn't it?" (on vacation at the hotel swimming pool)
- "It looks like it's going to be a good ski season with all the snow we've had lately. Is this your first time here?" (lift line)

After the initial question (his publicly recognizable face was really the environmental prop), I followed up with a declarative statement ("I always enjoyed seeing you in a role"), followed by two open-ended questions ("Tell me, how did you get into acting? Is it as hard as I've always heard?"). If it were you who sat next to this supporting actor, you also could have met him. So anytime and anywhere you want to meet someone:

Use the environment around you and find an environmental prop to cross the bridge *and* close the gap *between you and the person you decided to meet.*

Then:

Start a conversation either with a question, a declarative statement, or a combination of a question and a declarative statement.

And remember:

People are voice activated. You get them to speak to you by first speaking to them. Most people—even many celebrities—want to be friendly; they just need help getting started.

People are experts on their own life. And all experts like to talk about their area of expertise including their work. Acupuncturists, attorneys, scientists, massage therapists, physical trainers, accountants, doctors, gardeners, nurses, decorators, and computer programmers—most will gladly talk to you about their work because it's a way to talk to you about their life without getting too personal.

Yes, work is a great subject for small talk. Imagine the stories you might hear from art-gallery owners, restaurateurs, hotel managers, and flight attendants. What might you learn from an expert in photography, fishing, golf, tennis, art, music, history, cooking, yoga, or travel?

"You're a professional photographer? That sounds like a great job. How did you get into photography?" Or, "What kind of photography do you do?"

"What do you find helpful about yoga? I've been thinking about trying it for a long time."

"You own a pet shop?" (Using the echoing strategy, widen your eyes and have a rising, quizzical inflection in your voice.)

"Yes, I do."

"Wow, I can't imagine taking care of all those animals. It must be amazing to make a living this way. What's a typical day like in a pet shop?"

More Attention-getting Topics

Again, good conversational material includes TV shows, movies, sports, news events, and yes, scandals. There's always a scandal in the news. Andy Warhol made his famous prediction that in the future "everyone will have fifteen minutes of fame." I suspect today we are down to about fifteen seconds, but however long the fame lasts, the ones who have it are the subject of conversation for people at all levels of society—why not you?

Sports are natural conversation starters that interest millions of people. An estimated one hundred million people watch the Super Bowl. And don't overlook the potential in entertainment. Approximately forty million of us tune in to watch the Academy Awards, and Americans spend billions of dollars each year going to the movies. These are all great getting-to-know-you topics. Believe me when I tell you, you are a much more interesting conversationalist than you think you are.

Small talk is foreplay for deeper talk. It communicates, "You seem like an interesting person and I'd like to get to know you better." The trick is to be truly interested in other people instead of just trying to be interesting to them. If you show people you're interested in them, they'll generally find a way to become interested in you.

Yes, a conversation is a two-way street. Although the people you're talking with are equally responsible for the content and flow of the conversation, they may be one of the 90 percent of the population confused about the nature of small talk, and unsure what topics are appropriate. *Help these people out.*

Chapter 7

The Art of Listening

Aside from speaking, listening is the oldest and most often used interpersonal communication tool in the history of the world. Yet, even today, when the importance of education is unrelentingly a topic of conversation in our country, there are few programs that teach children how to listen. This is true even though most people we meet, more than anything, want to be heard. They want to be listened to.

From the moment children are born, parents begin teaching them how to speak.

- "Oh, honey, you are so beautiful. Say Mommy. I'm Mommy."
  - "What a gorgeous baby. This is Daddy! Say Daddy!"

Speech training continues through childhood:
- "Don't talk with food in your mouth."
- "Finish your sentence, sweetheart."
- "Tell the nice lady your name."
- "You know how old you are, darling. Tell the man how old you are."

Hundreds and hundreds of hours go into teaching a child to speak. Yet somehow, the art to listen is effectively lost.

The Importance of Listening and How to Do It Well

Hearing and listening are not the same. Hearing is an involuntary function of our auditory system. You don't have to work at it because it happens without any effort on your part. Listening on the other hand may appear to be passive, but it's an active skill that you have to work at. As you develop your listening skills, you will begin to hear interesting conversational topics that may have eluded you in the past, which you can now use to embellish future conversations. Conversations can and do feed on themselves and with a ferocious appetite. Often, all you have to do is listen.

Listening, however, is difficult for many people because we are born with the ability to think faster than others talk.

Behavioral scientists tell us the average person speaks at a rate of about one hundred to one hundred and fifty words a minute. But the one hundred billion nerve cells in our brain allow us to process words at the rate of three hundred and fifty to four hundred and fifty words per minute.

Yes, you read that right—our brains have one hundred billion nerve cells to process and transmit information and they do it rapidly. This discrepancy leaves us with a lot of spare time for doing other things besides listening. How we use that extra time goes a long way toward determining whether we are good or poor listeners.

Consider this: If people spoke at the rate of, say, one hundred and fifty words per minute, and the brain was programmed to listen at the same rate of speed, we wouldn't be able to do anything other than listen to the speaker. This one change would turn all of us into better listeners. But, because humans have this extra listening capacity, we can let our minds wander and silently talk to ourselves while others speak. But there is a conversational cost in doing this. You simply can't be a good conversationalist if you don't listen to the speaker fully and without distraction.

Imagine having a telephone conversation with someone on a crossed telephone line that forces you to hear another conversation while you are trying to have one yourself. It would be maddening. Yet for some people, this happens nearly all the time with face-to-face encounters. Those who are especially vulnerable are people so worried about what they're going to say next, they're formulating their responses while the other person is still speaking.

If this sounds like something you do, then please stop it immediately. The crossed conversational voice you hear is

Interesting

62

your own. By changing your focus on to what the other person is saying, rather than thinking about what you'll say next, you'll find you have more interesting comments and you'll make more friends in the process. People find it flattering to have others show an interest in what they have to say. Good listeners can tell of countless times they've had conversations and said virtually nothing; then, as they were parting company, the other person told them, "It was a pleasure talking with you."

Never listen to someone with the same passivity as you listen to the radio. The radio doesn't need feedback. People do.

An Oxymoron of Truth

As you probably know, an oxymoron is a combination of words that contradict each other, or words that go in opposite directions. We hear them all the time, yet we seldom question the discrepancy. People order **jumbo shrimp** in a restaurant or tell someone it's a **definite maybe**. They ask for an **unbiased opinion**, an **exact estimate**, and take out a **genuine imitation leather wallet**. People are even wearing **plastic glasses**!

So what's the point you might now be thinking? It's this, and though it is an oxymoron to be sure, it speaks truth. *People have to see that you're listening*. You show you're listening by giving your complete face-to-face attention and making eye contact with the person who is speaking. As humans we complete the communication circuit between speaker and listener with our eyes. Just as you won't get good reception from a satellite dish if it's facing in the wrong direction, you won't be a good conversationalist if you don't face the speaker. When you focus and maintain eye contact with someone who is talking to you, you're silently, but clearly, letting him know, "At this moment, you have my complete attention and nothing else in the world matters to me." The person speaking feels important, and that in turn encourages him to pay attention to you. Thus, both parties are more interested in the conversation and in each other.

Another reason we have allowed our listening skills to take a back seat on our communication highway is because listening is not as obvious a function as is speaking. Not only do others hear us when we speak, we also hear ourselves. We listen to what we are saying and judge our speech because we know everyone else is. But no one can hear us listen and it isn't on trial the way talking is. But that doesn't change the important reality that people don't want just to be heard. They want to be listened to as well.

Listening Tools

Nodding: In many cultures, nodding—that is, moving the head up and down—indicates affirmation, approval, acceptance, and understanding. What a wonderful compliment to offer your conversational partner without uttering a single word. Nodding is a gesture that encourages the speaker to continue talking. In fact, studies conducted by behavioral scientists confirm that people will talk three to four times longer when listeners nod their heads.

The opposite is also true. If you sit motionless with a blank expression on your face, the speaker is not encouraged to continue. *People have to see that you're listening.* Eye contact and nodding draw people out and reinforce the notion that you're interested in what they're saying and want to hear more.

In nodding, you become like an orchestra conductor. If you nod slowly and softly, nonverbally you communicate understanding and interest. On the other hand, if you nod your head rapidly while at the same time raising your hand and saying, **"Yes, yes,"** you're letting the speaker know you understand and would like the conversational ball tossed back to you.

"I've learned that people will forget what you said, people will forget what you did, but people will never forget how you made them feel." —Maya Angelou

Conversational Cues: Good conversationalists send both verbal and nonverbal cues. Here are some common ones that reinforce the message that you're listening:

Verbal		Non-Verbal
"That sounds right."	"I see what you mean."	Nodding
"Uh Huh."	"That's interesting."	Raised eyebrows
"Yes."	"Really."	Tilted head
"Hmmmm."	"Oh."	Look of surprise
"I agree."	"Wow!"	Smile
"That's great."	"Right."	Laugh

A good listener can ask questions with her eyes or with a tilt of her head. A good listener communicates even when she doesn't utter a word. Saying Julia is a good listener is the same as saying she is a good conversationalist and that makes her someone people like to be around. Keep in mind it's just as important to be interested in what others are saying as it is to be interesting to them.

What's the ultimate example of rapt attention? Picture kids sitting around a campfire, their eyes wide open and totally enthralled, as they listen to a camp counselor telling them a scary story. You, however, don't need to express that level of intensity when listening. Eye contact, nodding, facing the person squarely, a raised eyebrow, or a tilted head, combined with one or two verbal cue lines are all effective ways to send the right message.

Mirroring: When a person is telling you a story of how he got bad service in a restaurant and his expression becomes angry and he squints his eyes, you absolutely know that he's upset. His face and the irritated tone of his voice are unmistakable nonverbal conversational cues. As you listen, you may unconsciously frown or wrinkle your brow as a mirror-image response to his expressions. Similarly, you smile when someone says something funny. This mirroring tells the speaker you're listening. So, if you suspect you may be someone who maintains a stoic or expressionless face, consciously try to change that.

Let's assume someone excitedly says: **"Oh, I almost got killed today when I was crossing the street and a car ran a red light!"** Mirroring or copying the speaker's shocked expression, you say: **"Oh, that's terrible!"** instead of calmly and without much passion: "Oh, that's terrible." With your **mirrored** reaction, you're showing the sender that she conveyed her message effectively and that you received it. Without saying much, you said a lot. "I understand not only what you said, but also how you feel."

Empathy is identifying with and understanding another person's feelings. If you want to connect with people, this is an important skill. It's the ability to share feelings by mirroring their emotions, both verbally and nonverbally. It's not enough to have empathy—you also have to show it.

Getting a Word in Edgewise: We all know how annoying it is to have a conversation with someone who constantly interrupts us or changes subjects before we get a chance to finish expressing our thoughts. But we can learn two invaluable lessons of connectivity from such people. First, try not to interrupt, but always allow yourself to be *interruptible.* That's what good conversationalists do. Second, if you do need to interrupt because you have to make a point immediately, or you're concerned that you might forget to bring it up later, let the other person know you realize you're interrupting in one of the following ways:

• "Carol, please forgive me for interrupting you, but I want to say something I'm afraid I'll forget."

• "Carol, please forgive my interruption, but a thought just occurred to me that relates to what you were saying . . ."

First Impressions

You've heard the expression: "You never get a second chance to make a first impression." Yes, you do have to focus on how you present yourself when meeting people, but that's not enough. You also have to focus on the person you're meeting.

Say you met Anna at a party. While you're telling her a story about a funny, serious, or peculiar incident you were involved in, she periodically asks, "Tell me more about that . . . then what did you say? . . . What happened next?"

When you respond, she says, "Hmm . . . that's interesting." She smiles and nods when you say something clever and frequently says, "Really? . . . uh-huh . . . right."

What's your first impression of Anna? Probably a ten. You can do just as well. The benefits of honest listening are endless.

A shortcut to charm. Many people think great conversationalists are those who can talk interestingly about anything to anyone. Well, if you're like me, you may not be able to talk about everything to everybody, but you can train yourself to listen to anything from anyone. When you show an interest in what another person has to say, to them you become a more interesting person. It's a shortcut to charm, and one that requires little more than concentration—listening shows you're interested in a person and what he or she is saying.

Chapter 8

Ending Conversations Graciously

If you have difficulty ending a conversation with someone you just met, you're not alone. Many others also find it difficult. But of course, it's a different story when it comes to people you know well. Just as lots of people have no trouble starting a conversation with friends, family members, or people they work with, they also have little trouble ending a conversation with them, even abruptly.

"Steve, excuse me. I didn't realize the time. I'm late for an appointment—gotta run now."

We do that all the time with people we know without giving it a second thought. But for various reasons, many people have as much anxiety about ending a conversation with someone they just met as they do about starting one. This can be true whether the conversation lasts one minute or one hour. But regardless of the length of time, all conversations have to end. Here's how to end conversations graciously without awkwardness and in a way no one will feel hurt:

• One way to help rid yourself of the uneasiness about ending a conversation is to monitor your own feelings when someone you just met ends one with you. My guess is you won't see it as a traumatic experience. You might even admire the person for her self-confidence.

• Goodbyes should be short and sweet. Long, melodramatic, drawn-out goodbyes are neither required nor are they usually desired.

• Whether you're anxious or not, concentrate on ending the conversation in a warm and friendly manner. The tone you create prior to your departure is as important as the words you use. Good conversations, like good meals, should always end on a pleasant note.

Let's Get to It

Although there are guidelines for initiating conversations, there is no rigid formula for determining the best way to end one. It will depend in part on personal circumstances. Maybe you've run out of time, or given the particular social situation—say a party or trade show—you need to make the rounds.

However, there is one rule you should always follow when you feel the time has come to say goodbye: Never let your anxiety determine your action. If you want to end a conversation, you must take an active role in doing so. There is no short cut. The process involves both verbal and nonverbal communication. Just as conversational cues are used to open a conversation, they're also helpful in ending one.

In many Western cultures and certainly in the United States, the offer of a handshake is a well-known, nonverbal cue that a person is initiating the ritual of goodbye. The motion of extending your arm should be accompanied by a warm, friendly smile, eye contact, and a verbal expression suitable to the occasion.

Something we all know, but still worth mentioning. Handshakes are socially appropriate when:
- meeting someone
- parting from a face-to-face engagement
- congratulating a person
- thanking someone
- completing an agreement

If someone offers you his hand for any of the reasons indicated above, extend yours to complete the transaction. In Western cultures it is rude to reject someone's offer to shake your hand without a good reason. "Megan, I'm sorry—I can't shake your hand. I injured my wrist last week on the tennis court and it's still sore." (More about handshakes will be covered in Chapter 12.)

A Closer Look

Let's say you're at a party talking with a stranger when suddenly you make eye contact with someone you know. It's an old friend with whom you'd like to reconnect. If you're sitting, maintain eye contact with the person you've been talking with and slowly start to get up. Once standing, and at the appropriate moment, put out your arm to shake hands and say:

"Richie, I'm sorry. (warm smile) I see an old friend I need to talk to. It was great to meet you (offer hand) and I hope we can do it again soon."

"Richie, it was a pleasure talking about baseball with someone who knows the game so well. (offer hand) Hope we can do it again soon."

"Richie, I need to go now. (offer hand) It was actually fun to discuss politics with you. Thanks for the insights."

Sometimes you simply run out of time. Say you meet someone poolside while on vacation. It's almost lunchtime and you need to go. After glancing at your watch, you might say:

"René, I have to go back to my room and change. I hope I see you later."

Or you're at the gym. While you're talking to someone, the elliptical you've been waiting for opens up and you want to get to it before someone else does. You might say:

"Jeff, the machine I've been waiting for just opened up. I've got to go now, but I'll catch you later."

Imagine meeting someone on your lunch break.

"It's been nice talking with you, but I need to run. I have an errand to do."

"It's been nice talking with you, but I need to get back to work."

Even just this, "It's been nice talking with you, but I need to run," is usually sufficient.

Whatever words you use, don't forget to add a warm smile and friendly demeanor.

When Talk Is Tedious

You're at a social function and the person you just met is boring you. He's a chatterbox and the conversation is tedious. You want to end it, but how can you do this gracefully? Here's what to do: Simply restate a bit from the conversation to ease into a friendly close.

• "Marvin, I'll never forget your story about running into a bear on your hike. Thanks for sharing it. It was nice to meet you."

• "I hope I can remember that golf joke. It was really very funny. I enjoyed meeting you."

• "This was an insightful conversation. You sure know a lot about antiques."

• "I enjoyed meeting you. I hope everything works out."

• "This was a great conversation. Thanks for the advice—I'm going to get to those exercises tonight."

A word of caution. At a party, don't lie and say you have to go to the restroom, get a drink, or something to eat, implying that you will come back. When you don't return, the other person may feel slighted—and you'll feel uneasy because you know you weren't honest. Of course, if you're desperate, you can use one of these:

"Excuse me, I have to make a call. It was nice meeting you."

"Excuse me, I promised someone I would get back to her."

Runways

Everyone loves a "runway." Runways prepare people for what is about to happen. Some examples of life's runways:

• At the theater house lights dim before the curtain goes up

• In airports: "We will begin boarding in a few minutes"

• The snooze alarm that prepares us for the dreaded wake-up call

• At school: "Tomorrow there's a quiz on this week's work"

If you have a problem with goodbyes, runways offer a soft transition.

• "Danny, I'm going to have to go in a few minutes. I can't be late for my two o'clock appointment. I'll have to wind down our conversation now."

• "Harriet, I must be going in a few minutes, but please finish what you're saying. I want to hear how the story ends."

From time to time, you'll meet someone you want to meet again.

• "Rita, I've enjoyed our conversation, but it seems we won't have enough time to finish it. Maybe we can get together another time for a drink or coffee."

• "Joe, let's see if we can meet sometime in a few weeks. Okay if I give you a call?"

• "We seem to work in the same neighborhood. How about lunch one day next week?"

- "Leah, I'm glad I bumped into you. Let's exchange cards."
- "I'd like to continue our conversation later, Michael, if you're free."

Yes, all good things have to come to an end, even good conversations.

Go back and re-read the chapter again. Study the tips on saying goodbye. If circumstances permit, say them out loud. If you're reading this book in a public area with people nearby, mouth them silently. Try saying the words while offering your hand and smiling. Visualize various social settings. See yourself gracefully ending conversation. And don't forget to monitor your own reactions when people take the initiative in ending a conversation with you. Knowing that your feelings weren't hurt will help you take a similar initiative with others in the future.

Chapter 9

When You Smile, the World Smiles, Too

"You shouldn't judge a book by its cover."

vs.

"You never get a second chance to make a first impression."

The first statement, "You shouldn't judge a book by its cover," does not describe the behavior of most people in this country. The evidence is clear, almost unequivocal, that people not only do judge a book by its cover, but in our society, in our culture, and maybe in the whole world, people seem to have a need to size up others rather quickly. There is a lot of scientific evidence to indicate that we actually come hard-wired into the world this way.

How Quick?

Interpersonal, face-to-face communication experts don't completely agree on how long it takes to make a first impression. The amount of time seems to range from five seconds to five minutes. After studying this subject for a number of years, I have come to my own conclusion. It doesn't matter whether it takes five seconds or five minutes. What is important to know is that the process begins immediately, even before you speak. So if it begins immediately, then that's when you should begin making a favorable first impression, from the very first second. What comes before speaking? Your smile—or lack of one.

Social scientists tell us that a smile is the clearest, least confusing, and most universally used and understood communication signal in the world. The fastest and most immediate way to allow people you're meeting for the first time to feel relaxed and comfortable in your presence is to greet them with a smile. When two people meet and exchange smiles, they create a bond that would not exist without that smile. In effect, your smile says:

- "I'm a friendly person. You can relax and feel safe with me."
- "You seem to be a person I'm going to like and, at the very least, I feel safe and comfortable in your presence."
- "I'm glad to meet you."

What an important and necessary message to send someone you're meeting for the first time, second time, third time, or . . . anytime in the future!

Note: Before we go further, I want to alert you to the fact that I'm talking about a specific smile. The smile I'm referring to is a "heartfelt, teeth-showing smile." Any other smile won't work nearly as well. As human beings, we have all kinds of smiles. For example:

- A slight smile
- A "cat that ate the canary" smile, sometimes known as "a shit-eating grin"
- A mischievous smile
- A sneer or a smirk smile
- A smile that might accompany sarcasm
- An embarrassed smile*

*Many people instinctively offer an embarrassed smile when caught doing something harmless, but socially wrong. For example, a cashier waves a one-dollar bill in the air he just received from a customer to pay a $4 tab. The customer, thinking she handed the cashier a $5 bill, responds with an embarrassed smile that acknowledges the error and, at the same time, allows her to show her innocence without having to explain.

"Oh, please, don't ask me to say cheese!"

You know how hard it is to smile when someone is taking your picture. You feel your smile looks phony. And you feel that way because probably it does. The reason forced or on-demand smiles look and feel unreal is because they are unreal. What's missing is the emotion, something that makes us feel happy enough to smile.

I'm going to give you three tricks professionals use to make a full, heartfelt smile, not only look real, but also make it feel real. First, though, I need to say something to the guys. Most men will need to work a little harder to develop a teeth-showing smile than women will. Women seem to be born with the ability to allow their upper lip to pull back and up when they smile and even when talking. It's a natural neurological phenomenon that makes for a more pleasant initial meeting and conversation.

Now, here's the first professional trick I promised you. As you read the following, don't just read the words, act them out through self-visualization.

Pretend you're out in a public area and bump into a friend you haven't seen in years—someone you used to hang out with and have wonderful memories of your times together. A great big, heartfelt, teeth-showing smile lights up your face.

"Robin, what a great surprise. It's been at least ten years since I saw you. You look great!"

"Jay, oh my gosh, it is you! Wow. I'm so glad to see you again."

Or, pretend you are meeting a famous celebrity, athlete, politician, entertainer, or actor. Besides being well-known, this is a person you like and admire.

"(full name of famous person), what a pleasure to meet you."

Reproduce the heartfelt, teeth-showing smile you would undoubtedly have when running into an old friend or being in the presence of a famous person and the smile you make will look real. For a few days, practice using this smile when you greet people and soon you'll have turned what had been your consciously deliberate and purposefully cheerful smile into an authentic one. Of course, I don't mean a fawning or subservient smile. This smile is one that says, "I'm thrilled to meet you."

The second trick toward perfecting a heartfelt, teeth-showing smile is to allow your cheeks to rise upward toward your eyes when you smile. If you're a little confused or think this is silly, let me explain why. Smiling is a perfect example of cause and effect. It is very difficult if not impossible to smile and not feel happy, even if you're "faking" the smile.

Why? When you execute a teeth-showing smile and simultaneously allow your cheeks to move upward toward your eyes, the muscular activity causes the brain to release endorphins into your system. Endorphins are natural body chemicals that scientists refer to as the happy hormones. You will actually feel happy, even though you may have faked the smile. It's the endorphins.

Equally as important is that everyone who looks at you will feel happy as well. Why? Research tells us it's almost impossible to look at someone who is smiling at you and not smile back. If someone greets you with a heartfelt, teeth-showing smile, you'll likely return the smile. The smile you both make releases endorphins in each of you, making you both feel happy and at ease with each other.

So people will feel relaxed in your presence either because you seem friendly as a result of your smile, or they'll put themselves at ease because of their own smile. In most cases, it will be a combination of both. Without knowing why, people will tell themselves they were happy to have met you. And thanks to those happy hormones, the endorphins, they really were.

To prove the point and also to encourage you to work on an authentic smile, try this. Give yourself a big teeth-showing smile. Let those cheeks rise and allow your eyes to sparkle. Hold the smile and gleam in your eyes and try to think of something negative. Something that would make you feel sad or angry. Really try. Don't be too surprised when you can't. You are hard-wired this way. We all are. Scientists tell us that there are compatible responses and incompatible responses. Smile and you can't be sad or angry. *Those happy hormones, the endorphins, won't let you.*

The opposite is also true. Frown and you can't be happy. Here's how you can put that to a test: Put a frown or scowl on your face by tightening your lips, squinting your eyes, and furrowing your brow. Now, try to feel happy. Think of some happy event or something that made you laugh. Don't be surprised if you find it almost impossible to come up with happy thoughts while you have a frown on your face. It's another example of an incompatible response and yet more evidence about how important it is to smile when you meet anyone for the first time and every time thereafter.

Another reason to smile. It's very difficult to get people to like you when you don't like them. Of course, actors on screen or the stage can convince you they like someone. They do this by creating an alter-ego inside themselves and then they become that character, feeling it as if it were real. But they have to spend a lot of time becoming someone else, so they can make it real. You, on the other hand, can make it look and feel real with very little work or rehearsing on your part. And how? Again, the answer is by smiling—

81

a great big, heartfelt, teeth-showing smile. The feed-back effect from the endorphins will make you feel that you like the person you're meeting. You just will. This is so simple and it works. Perfect your heartfelt, teeth-showing smile and the world will become warmer and friendlier because the people you meet will become warmer and friendlier to you. It's human nature that people like people who like them. This isn't an over-simplification—it's very profound, and many scientific studies have proven it. People do like people who like them. Even the most self-confident people are a bit anxious about being accepted when they meet some-one for the first time. By smiling at them, you validate their self-confidence.

Here is the third trick I promised you to perfect your heartfelt, teeth-showing smile into a perfectly wonderful, natural one.

Millions and millions of people enter stores every day in America to shop. The store clerks and/or cashiers are just a few feet away from the people they serve. Yet most customers treat them as if they don't exist. In the future, smile and say hello before ordering or, as you are about to hand over your credit card or money for what you just purchased, acknowledge them. It will help *make their day*. Greeting and talking to the anonymous people you encounter every day, but perhaps previously ignored, will hone your interpersonal, face-to-face communication reflexes, and make you a better meeting-peo-ple-for-the-first-time conversationalist. In the process, you'll make these people feel happier. You'll see how many peo-ple will respond if you greet them with a warm, teeth-showing smile and a "Good morning." Additionally, while you're making people feel good about the moment they spent with you, you'll end up getting back more than you gave. All your cumulative warm, teeth-showing smiles are releasing endorphins and making your day more pleasant. So, do it consciously to get started. Do it until it becomes a reflex action. Soon it will become a reflex action.

Let's stop for a minute and talk in general about the different messages a smile communicates.

• We generally respond more favorably to a smile from someone of the opposite sex, even when there is no sexual connotation to the smile. Yes guys, women do respond more favorably to a man smiling at her, as opposed to another woman. This, of course, is absolutely true with men—a man responds *much* more favorably to a woman who smiles at him, as opposed to a man.

• People generally respond more eagerly to a smile from someone of a higher social status than from those on an equal one. For example, if you pass a celebrity in the street, or an important elected politician at a function, and you make eye contact, chances are if you're like most people, you're going to offer a jubilant smile. The person of importance, if polite, will probably acknowledge your greeting with a slight smile, and an "eyebrow flash" perhaps accompanied by a gentle waving of the hand to indicate acknowledgment. (An eyebrow flash is a single up and down movement of the eyebrows that implies recognition.) Although an eyebrow flash may not be equal in its presentation to a broad smile, most people will be delighted with the response.

• On the job, many people try not to smile unless it's part of their work. They want to show they're serious about what they do, which they think translates into control and competency. If you're one of the non-smilers on the job, okay, you made your point. But so what! Don't you want people to want to work with you? Is it so bad to be a competent *and* well-liked co-worker? You can accomplish this by doing your job diligently, while at the same time greeting and interacting with your co-workers with a pleasant smile. Even if you're the boss, the people who report to you are your co-workers. What's wrong with people going home and telling their friends and family that they have a great boss?—someone who is a pleasure to work with. How can that be bad for business?

• Another well-researched phenomenon. When you begin an encounter with a smile and the other person smiles back, the encounter will generally last longer. In my personal experience, I observe this regularly and so will you if you pay attention to it yourself. Imagine you see someone you know coming toward you in a shopping mall. If you exchange slight smiles or no smile at all, the chances are you'll both keep walking. On the other hand, if both of you exchange a warm, heartfelt, teeth-showing smile, you will, in all probability, stop and chat for a minute. The smile all by itself will slow each of you down to meet and talk, even if briefly.

• People who smile are judged to be more attractive, pleasant, sociable, sincere, and confident than those who don't. Why confident? Smiling gives you an aura of being comfortable in your own skin, at ease with yourself and the world. Go to a party and walk around looking glum and you come off as someone with no confidence. If you smile and look relaxed, people will assume you have a lot of self-confidence. Confidence comes from the inside, but you show it on the outside.

• When wishing someone well or offering congratulations, don't forget the heartfelt, teeth-showing smile. At least as much as the words you use, the smile will externalize your inner feelings of joy for the person you're congratulating.

• Smiling lifts the face and adds youthfulness to it. (Look around and notice when elderly people offer a great big smile how much younger they look.)

• Smile when you see a neighbor. It's good practice, and you'll develop a terrific reputation in your neighborhood. I once had a neighbor named John who was always smiling. Someone asked me about him, and I said, "Oh, he's a terrific guy, a nice guy." Then, it occurred to me that I hardly knew John. My rave review was all based on his smile and how it made me feel.

• Let's get a little bit deeper into this transaction of exchanging smiles with someone when you meet. Smiling will encourage people to like you, which will lead them to trust you. Like and trust are first cousins; we generally don't like people we don't trust, and we tend to trust people we do like.

This, in turn, will make it easier for people to want to listen to and be more open to what you're telling them. It will also make it easier and more comfortable for them to open up a bit more to you than they might normally do. It's astonishing to think that this change of attitude can all start with your smile. But it can and does.

Boy, did they get it right.
When you're smilin' . . . keep on smilin'
The whole world smiles with you
And when you're laughin' . . . keep on laughin'
The sun comes shining through

But when you're cryin' . . . you bring on the rain
So stop your frownin' . . . be happy again
Cause when you're smilin' . . . keep on smilin'
The whole world smiles with you

WHEN YOU'RE SMILING
Words and Music by MARK FISHER, JOE GOODWIN
and LARRY SHAY
Copyright © 1928 (Renewed) EMI MILLS MUSIC INC.
and MUSIC BY SHAY
Exclusive Print Rights for EMI MILLS MUSIC INC.
Administered by ALFRED MUSIC PUBLISHING CO., INC.

Chapter 10

The Art of Giving and Receiving Compliments

"I can live for two months on a good compliment."
— Mark Twain

A compliment is a brief social transaction that, like a beautiful sunset, doesn't last long but leaves a memorable impression. The ability to give a sincere compliment is a gift, and it relates directly to the laws of connectivity. We all appreciate being told we're special, and we like those who make us feel that way.

Compliments, if sincere and genuine, have an immediate bonding effect. During a conversation:

"You have a wonderful sense of humor."

"You certainly are a fabulous dancer."

"I really like how you decorated your home."

"You did a super job on that project. It was so clear and concise."

"What terrific kids you're raising."

"Is that a new outfit? It looks amazing on you!"

When used as an environmental prop, a compliment can also be an appropriate conversational ice breaker:

"You play a great game of tennis."

"Your dog is so cute!"

"That was a terrific question you asked in class tonight."

"You're getting quite a tan this summer."

"That is such a beautiful ring."

Receiving a Compliment

Many people seem uncomfortable to be on the receiving end of a compliment. If that's you, please pay attention: A compliment is a gift and you should accept it as one. Just as you'd send an e-mail or note thanking someone who gave you a gift, you have the same obligation to acknowledge a compliment. Just as you wouldn't downplay a gift, don't downplay a compliment. "Oh, you shouldn't have. Here, please take this gift back." If that sounds ridiculous, it's because it is.

Have you ever heard this curious dialogue?

"That's an attractive sweater."

"Oh, this old thing."

This is no time for modesty. Fulfill your obligation. Make eye contact, smile, and with a warm, friendly tone in your voice say, "Thank you." It's a sign of <u>social intelligence</u>.

A compliment is not an exchange. You not only don't have to return a compliment, you shouldn't. These examples illustrate how a follow-up remark can detract from the compliment you received.

"Your golf game is terrific."

"Oh, you're not so bad yourself."

"You made an important point in class tonight."

"So did you last week."

Let me correct myself. As we know, there always seems to be an exception to the rule. <u>If you think the person who complimented you deserves more than a simple thank you, consider the following responses expressed sincerely.</u>

"Your golf game is terrific."

"You made my day. Thank you for saying that."

"You made an important point in class tonight."

"Oh, thank you. That means a lot to me."

In each case, you did return the compliment, but in a meaningful way.

Opportunities to Compliment

Asking someone's opinion, commenting favorably about something said, and acknowledging that a person knows a lot about a certain subject are all appropriate compliments.

- "That's so interesting. Tell me more about that."
- "I never thought of that. That's a terrific way to look at it."
- "You have a fascinating point of view."
- "I'm impressed by how much you know about . . ."

Sincerity counts. Always keep in mind that compliments must sound sincere. It's not enough for you to know they're sincere; the person on the receiving end has to know it as well.

Let's consider other subjects that might lead to a compliment. And not just to strangers, but to friends or family members.

- **Fitness**

Fitness demands hard work. It takes energy, time, and discipline. Telling someone he looks fit acknowledges his effort, and it's especially appreciated by people who have lost weight.

"Wow, it looks like you lost a lot of weight and you look great! How did you do it?"

If he has lost weight and wants to talk about it, let him. He will appreciate it, and it will enhance your relationship.

- **Someone's boyfriend or girlfriend**

"Judy, it was great to meet Adam last week. He seems like such a great guy. You make a perfect couple."

- **Furnished home or apartment**

"Wendy, what a beautiful home you have."

- **Neat work area**

"Denise, I'm always so impressed by how neat and organized you are. I would love to be like that."

- **Children**

It's hard to overstate the impact you'll have if you can sincerely compliment someone's child.

"Vicki, I can't get over how charming your daughter is."

"Doug, I'm always impressed by how well you get along with your little boy."

- **Someone's age**

"You're kidding! You look ten years younger than that."

Young or old. The marvel of this compliment is that it's appreciated by all ages. In our society, older people are trying to look younger while younger people are trying to look older. Appreciation of the following compliment will equal the level of effort that person put into trying to look younger or older. So, "You're kidding! I would never have guessed your age," is quite a compliment to just about everyone.

Be specific. The best compliment is not about what a person is wearing or doing, but rather a compliment that is connected directly to the person. For example, there's nothing wrong with a compliment about a thing: "That's a terrific looking suit." But better still is a compliment that targets the object and the person at the same time.

- "Lee, you have great taste. You look terrific in that suit."
- "That's a beautiful picture. Cindy, you're so good at spotting wonderful art."
- "A delicious dish, Abby. I would love to cook as well as you do."
- "Ilana, a wonderful party. You really have being a good hostess down pat."
- "Gerri, I loved that story you told. You have a real talent for words."
- "That sounds like good advice. James. You always come up with the right answer. You're great that way."

Often when you make people feel good about themselves, they'll have an emotional investment to live up to the compliment you gave them.

- "You're so organized."
- "You're always so upbeat and full of energy."
- "You have a great smile."
- "You're an amazing swimmer."

Then, when the recipient meets you, or even thinks about you, she'll associate those good feelings with you. If you want to be valued, then give value.

Even silent admiration can be taken as a compliment. In any city in this country, hardly a day passes that you can't witness a number of men doing a "body twist" or a "neck twist" as they pass a woman they think is attractive. Many guys twist the upper part of their body and neck nearly completely around to get one last look, which reminds me of a quote from an old-time, frank-speaking movie star, Mae West: "It is better to be looked over than overlooked."

History has value. Remembering prior events, or subjects you talked about in previous conversations, creates a lasting impression. It lets people know that you, not only listened, but also cared enough to remember what they said. It's an implied compliment and one of the laws of connectivity that will bring people closer to you.

- "How's your kid brother these days? He's going to graduate college this year, isn't he?"
- "Are you enjoying that new car you bought last year?"
- "How was your trip to Europe?"
- "I remember the last time we met, you were telling me about your plans to _____."

Referencing a past conversation takes concentration and practice, but it pays dividends. It's a way of turning casual acquaintances into friends. As an indication of how powerful a technique this is, note your own reaction when someone does it with you.

- "Elizabeth, the last time we talked, you said _____."
- "Pete, I thought a lot about what you told me the last time we met concerning _____."

Wouldn't you feel impressed?

Most people will internalize these remarks and conclude that you take what they say seriously. They'll bask in the warmth of knowing you respect them. The ability to boost someone's self-esteem is a powerful gift.

Even if the moment has passed, it's never too late to revisit: "Sondra, just a few minutes ago you said something that interested me and I'd like to hear more about it." Who wouldn't enjoy hearing a request like that?

Rarity has value. An aside for my female readers:

In our culture most of the time it's men who compliment women:

- "You look beautiful tonight."
- "I love the way you look in that dress."
- "I suppose I'm not the first guy to tell you that you have beautiful eyes."

As to giving a compliment to a man, ask any of your male friends and they will probably admit that just having a woman smile at them is a compliment all by itself. An even greater compliment in a man's eyes is to have a woman ask his advice—and then listen attentively to what he has to say. Doing so will build his self-esteem and trust me, it will make his day.

Congratulations!

Any time you have a chance to say congratulations to someone, say it. Give this person your full attention. Make eye contact. Square off. Have a smile on your face and in your voice. Use your whole arsenal of listening and conversational tools. Ask lots of questions and you'll earn a fortune in gratitude and friendship. Here are some obvious opportunities to offer your congratulations:

- "I just got engaged."
- "My daughter is getting married."

- "I'm graduating from college."
- "I just bought a new home."
- "I got a promotion at work."
- "I got a new job."

Compliments are free. Use them wisely and often when the opportunity arises. But remember, always be sincere.

Chapter 11

The Language of Eye Contact

Most communication experts agree that eye contact is not far behind language as a powerful means of communication. Without speaking, the eyes can express a wide range of feelings including:

Admiration	Awe
Boredom	Wonder
Amazement	Curiosity
Fascination	Respect
Fear	Joy

There is clear evidence that simply by maintaining a lot of eye contact, you can increase the chances that someone will like you. Michael Argyle, a noted psychologist who taught at Oxford University, determined that people look at each other during a conversation 30 to 60 percent of the time. When one person looks at the other more than 60 percent of the time, it's a sure sign of interest. Of course, when you're interested in the other person, chances are you're also interested in what he or she has to say. People do feel flattered when people maintain eye contact with them when they're speaking. It does show interest.

Too Much, Too Little and Just Right

Please don't confuse eye contact with staring. The best eye contact occurs when two people look at each other in a soft mutual gaze. A fixed, unbroken gaze though is staring and just about everyone finds that unsettling. People who stare inappropriately may be regarded as rude or even threatening. Stare at the wrong person in the wrong place and you could find yourself in big trouble.

Only young children can stare without appearing rude. Of course, as they grow older, their parents will teach them not to stare. Most people become embarrassed when caught staring at someone and often apologize for this breach of etiquette by offering a half smile. It communicates, "Oops!"

On the other hand, too little eye contact can communicate that you are:
- Not paying attention
- Insincere or dishonest ("Look me straight in the eye when you say that")

- Sad or depressed
- Defeated
- Shy

People who are shy may also be very warm and make charming partners, companions, dates, or colleagues. But because of their shyness, they may at first have trouble maintaining eye contact. It doesn't necessarily mean they don't have good feelings toward you. They may simply find it hard to express those feelings, even in non-verbal body language.

When a person avoids or withdraws eye contact, others can view it as a sign of dislike. Then again, it could also mean the opposite. We don't want to get caught staring at someone of the opposite sex because it can be an indication of sexual attraction. Take a budding office romance. How many times has one woman in the office said to another woman, "Of course, he likes you. Can't you see the way he looks at you?" Or to a man, "Of course, she likes you. Can't you see the way she doesn't look at you?" It works both ways.

Like greeting cards, the eyes send a variety of messages:
They were eyeball-to-eyeball
A look that could kill
An evil eye
Bedroom eyes
Giving someone the eye
He looked at me knowingly
He couldn't look me straight in the eye

What you should know about the eyes and eye contact:

• Even public speaking is a two-way communication process that requires eye contact. Accomplished public speakers know that they must make eye contact with members of the audience in order to "build a bridge" between them and their listeners.

• When talking on the telephone, people gesture and focus their eyes in approximately the same way they do while having a face-to-face conversation.

• Squinting the eyes and furrowing the brow can communicate that the other person:

  • Can't hear you
  • Is interested in what you're saying
  • Is confused by what you're saying

• You can trespass with your eyes. For example, a man staring at a woman's body too often or too long can upset her and make her uncomfortable. Of course, if it's a man she knows and cares for, this becomes a compliment.

• People blink unconsciously about twenty times a minute, less when relaxed and more when under stress or in an aroused or excited state. It's part of our primatology, being human. This means on average people blink their eyes seven million-plus times a year. Assuming the average person gets eight hours of sleep, let's do the math.

About 20 Blinks each minute X 60 minutes = 1,200 blinks per hour.

1200 blinks per hour X 16 hours = 19,200 blinks per day.

19,200 blinks per day X 365 days = 7,008,000 blinks per year.

One of the functions of blinking is that it lubricates the eye with moisture secreted by the tear duct. The more intense we are when reading or working on the computer, the less we blink. The less we blink, the less the eyes are lubricated leading to dryness that in turn makes our eyes feel tired.

• A wink is not a blink. A wink in our country is a gesture generally used to indicate interest in another person. It can also mean:

"What I'm about to say is between us."

"What I'm about to say is just a joke. Don't take it seriously."

• When people are afraid, their eyes appear frozen open, as if not to miss the slightest sign of danger.

• When people feel anger, contempt, or disgust, their eyes narrow into slits. Other nonverbal signs that might accompany this include furrowing the brow, grinding the teeth, and clenching the fists.

• When we look at something we find attractive, the pupils of our eyes can expand to become 45 percent larger than normal. It's as though the eyes want to take in as much as possible of the attractive sight.

• In a reverse pattern, tests show that when people look at photographs of men and women that are identical except one has been altered to make the pupils look larger, people invariably prefer the ones with larger pupils. This is equally true whether for women looking at a man's picture or vice versa.

• Parents sometimes use unflinching eye contact to maintain dominance over misbehaving children. The love is there, but so is the message: "Don't make me more upset than I am now or you'll be punished."

• While an upward glance and eye-rolling usually convey exasperation, they can also communicate disagreement or disbelief about what was said or done. Without uttering a single word, the person makes a clear statement: "I can't believe you said that."

• Looking below the bridge of the nose and letting the eyes linger on the mouth is flirtatious and sends an unmistakable message of sexual attraction. If that is what you intend to signal, okay, but just know what you're doing because it will probably either end the conversation or intensify it.

To Improve Your Eye Contact

At the very least, eye contact communicates confidence. There's no substitute for looking a person in the eye, smiling sincerely, and saying, "Hey, it's nice to meet you." However, it isn't unusual to have a problem with eye contact. If you're among those who do, here are some suggestions that will make it easier:

• Without crowding the person you're talking with, lean forward very slightly. This posture will help you maintain eye contact. When you make eye contact this way, you draw people into your world.

• You may hear you can improve eye contact during a conversation by focusing on the person's eyes to determine their color. I don't think it's necessary to go to this extreme. Instead, simply make casual eye contact by targeting the area from the bridge of the nose up to and around the eyebrows. It's fine to look away now and then for a brief time and in fact it will relieve any stress either of you might feel from too much eye contact. But of course, be careful not to switch your focus to someone or something else in your immediate surroundings.

• Another tip you can use with children, boyfriends, girlfriends, spouses, or anyone else who is special to you is to prolong eye contact briefly *as you are saying goodbye.* Even one extra second sends the unmistakable message that this person matters to you. And if the look is accompanied by a warm, bright smile, the person may even see you as, yes, charismatic.*

*Charisma is a special quality of charm, personal appeal, and magnetism.

"The eyes are the pioneers that first announce the soft tale of love." —Propertius

Eye contact is one of the most subtle, yet effective forms of communication that allows two people to meet without an introduction. In the United States, men and women differ in the way they use eye contact to draw a romantic interest into their world. Among heterosexuals, women, once they have met a man, tend to maintain eye contact longer than men do. But men, more than women, employ eye contact as a tool to meet women. Women, rethink your strategy. Be aware of the enormous power you can have over a man you're interested in meeting if you give him a knowing and slightly lingering look, one that leans more toward friendliness than sexuality. A look like that can be as effective as offering a bone to a hungry puppy. But keep in mind that if you then avert your eyes, most men will take that as a sign of rejection. And some people still say it's still a man's world!

"One of the most wonderful things in nature is a glance of the eye; it transcends speech." —Emerson

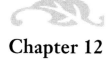

Chapter 12

Coming to Grips with Handshakes

At some point in a book on interpersonal, face-to-face communications, a few comments and observations on handshakes are a must. I mentioned in Chapter 8 (Ending Conversations) how extending your arm for a handshake can serve as an effective nonverbal signal when:

Meeting someone   Thanking someone
Congratulating a person   Ending a conversation
Completing an agreement ("Let's shake on that.")

Evolutionary social scientists tell us that in the earliest days when our ancestors started to explore the world beyond the area where they were born, they developed a custom that might explain how shaking hands came about. This action was used as a response to an unexpected face-to-face encounter with strangers from another part of their continent, who had also gone out exploring.

The leaders of each tribal group would stop and, at a safe, but communicable distance, straighten and extend their arms out at shoulder-height with their palms open and facing the leader of the other tribe. This showed their intention to communicate friendliness and intention not to be hostile or threatening to the opposing tribe.

Today, a handshake may seem like a perfunctory ritual, but as with a good conversation, there are rules of the road you need to be aware of. Social psychologists tell us that a handshake communicates a lot about who you are as a person when people first meet you.

Handshake Rules of the Road

• **Practice the ideal US handshake.** In this country, the preferred handshake takes place when you nudge the web of your hand into the web of the person's hand you are shaking. The web is the V area of your hand between your thumb and the finger next to it, the index finger. In addition to leaving a strong impression, it helps you avoid receiving the Bone Crusher or the Limp Wrist, both annoying handshakes.

• **Add a name to your handshake to create a social connection.** Research tells us there is a 75 percent better chance of people remembering you and your name if you shake hands with them and simultaneously say your name. Similarly, you also have a 75 percent better chance of remembering the other person's name if, when shaking hands, you both say your names.

• **Meet and greet more than one person.** At times, you'll likely find yourself at an event where a friend or business associate introduces you to a group of three or four people. Although the following may take some determination and practice to develop, trust me, it's worth the effort. Square off and maintain eye contact with each person as you shake his or her hand *before* turning to the next person. Turning your head to look at the next person before you finish shaking someone's hand reduces the importance you place on that introduction. This is definitely not the impression you want to leave or how you want to make people feel about themselves. However silly this may sound, not squaring off may be interpreted as a signal that you're giving someone a "cold shoulder." It's a well-known form of body language and part of our vernacular that communicates, at the very least, you don't take the person seriously.

"Hey, did you enjoy meeting Marvin?"

"I don't know. He gave me the cold shoulder."

And remember, whether shaking hands one-on-one or in a group, eye contact and a handshake go together.

• **Women offering their hand:** There are a lot of men in this country who are still not sure if they should offer a handshake to a woman. And so women, you need to take the lead here. Whether it's in a business or social setting, if you know it is one in which men would shake hands, graciously offer your hand without hesitation. I'm talking about an assertive, firm, warm handshake that says, "I'm glad to meet you." In offering your hand freely, you'll score a lot of points with men. It takes them off the hook and eliminates their dilemma.

Research tells us that women who easily offer a firm handshake make a more favorable impression than women who offer a soft, so-called feminine handshake *or none at all.* And surprising as it may seem, this also holds true when two women meet. The woman who might have felt uncertain about initiating a handshake will have a positive impression of confidence and self-assurance about the woman who did.

In the evolution of women's rights and the protocol of handshakes, we currently seem to have things reversed. Centuries ago, it was common when a man greeted a woman for him to kiss the lady's hand. But *only* if the woman first offered her hand. Yes, you read that right. A man wasn't allowed to kiss the lady's hand unless the lady first offered her hand. As a man, I wonder why they didn't keep this feminine right in the NOW* Statement of Purpose. Today a hand kiss, if at all, will be initiated by the man as a romantic gesture to the woman he's attached to, or as a flirting gesture with a woman he's interested in becoming attached to.

The National Organization for Women founded in 1966 to bring about and maintain equality for all women.

• **"So what did you say you did for a living?"** Sometimes, life presents us with a contradiction of what we have been taught to believe. We think of a Limp Finger or Dead Fish handshake as wimpy and showing a lack of confidence or interest in meeting people. But that's not always true. Many people use their hands for a living or hobby and understand- ably take care to protect them. In fact, oftentimes surgeons, dentists, musicians, artists, costume jewelers, custom tailors, and others prefer not to shake hands at all. Even so, being socially savvy most will, but often as briefly and softly as possible.

So, don't be quick to judge if someone you just met shakes your hand this way. If the initial greeting turns to small talk and you get the opportunity to ask about the person's profession, you might discover the reason behind that Dead Fish handshake.

Like compliments (See Chapter 10), handshakes should generally be delivered with an inner attitude of warmth and sincerity.

Chapter 13

Conversational Pitfalls to Avoid

Oftentimes people use repetitive words and expressions that get in the way of meaningful conversations. I call these "conversational pitfalls" and if you're among those with this habit, I urge you to pay close attention. Once you become aware of what the pitfalls are and how to overcome them, you'll see you can do so quickly and it will make every conversation you have a better one. The place to start is here and the time is now.

Pitfall Number One: Lazy Talk

Lazy Talk expressions are generally clichés and fillers that form speech patterns we repeat so often, we don't hear ourselves doing this. But other people hear them clearly. I don't want to be harsh, but frankly, if you give into Lazy Talk, you will diminish the image you likely want to convey. In fact, any time people slip into Lazy Talk, they might as well wear a sign that says: "I'm not a sophisticated conversationalist."

Here are typical examples of Lazy Talk:

- "I went to the movies, *you know*, and saw _____, *you know*. It was, *you know*, a very funny movie, *you know*."
- "*Like*, I went to the party and everyone was *like* having a good time. Except, *like* this one guy who was *like* . . ."
- "Do you get my drift?"
- "Etc., etc., etc."
- "Whatever."
- "You know what I mean?"
- "Do you know what I'm saying?"
- "And-so-on and so-forth."
- "Stuff like that."
- "This, that, and the other thing."

Most people wouldn't go out in public inappropriately dressed. So, why repeatedly dress your conversation in words and expressions such as "whatever," "do you get my drift," or "stuff like that"? The need to cure Lazy Talk habits is compelling. Until people rid themselves from these patterns of "non-talk," they simply can't be communicatively attractive. To overcome the habit of Lazy Talk, you'll need to get someone to help you. Ask a person you trust—a spouse, a close friend, or even a co-worker—if you have a problem with this and if so, what expressions you unwittingly use. Brace yourself for the answer, but take heart. I'm now going to show you what you can do to break the habit.

Habit-breaking Techniques

Most long-established habits, such as smoking, nail-biting, even chewing gum, are hard to shake. This isn't the case with Lazy Talk. For self-motivated people, it's a relatively quick fix and one that works every time. However, you must be willing to endure the discomfort of annoying yourself in the short term, so you can stop annoying others in the long term.

First, don't procrastinate—start immediately. It takes some work, but not much. The real requirements are focus, persistence, and a strong desire to improve. Make a pact with the person helping you. Each time you lapse into Lazy Talk, the "coach" must tell you immediately. "You just said, *you know*" or "You just said, *like*." At first you may deny saying those words. Remember, most people don't hear themselves saying *"you know"* or *"like."* That's why you need a coach. But after being alerted a few times, *you will* become conscious of what you're doing. Once you've turned that corner and if you stick with it on a persistent basis, you'll quickly overcome this bad habit.

If you have close friends who frequently use Lazy Talk expressions, ask them if they would like help getting rid of this annoying habit. Don't be surprised if they, like you, deny the problem. You might even get this response: "*Like* Randall what are you talking about? *Like* I wouldn't think about talking like that, *you know what I mean?*"

Pitfall Number Two: Speech Disfluencies

Disfluency (also spelled dysfluency) may be a word you've never heard before, but it represents something familiar to all of us. Speech disfluencies are words or expressions injected into conversation that interrupt a smooth flow or that are inconsistent with the meaning or purpose of the message.

For example the two words *"Um"* and *"Uh"* may appear to be virtually identical. But one is disfluency and the other is not. In life, we hear these two words differently—and I am not just splitting hairs. There actually is a difference between *Um* and *Uh*. Using the word *"Um"* on occasion is the brain's way of buying you time, while you collect your thoughts or find the right word.

"What was the name of that restaurant in Rome you liked so much?"

"Oh yeah, it was...um...Romano Buon Appetito."

"Uh," however, is speech disfluency and as such is a bad habit. The duration of time between *"uh"* and the next word is invariably short because the brain isn't engaged in thinking about the next word.

"So, *uh*, what, *uh*, did you think of the new restaurant you went to last night? How, *uh*, was the food?"

"Uh" is a form of Lazy Talk—it has to go.

Pitfall Number Three: If and But

Let's say you're in a situation in which you have just done something that makes the other person uncomfortable. An apology on your part is called for—and you may be tempted to start it with the word *"if."* It is best to avoid doing that, as

I'll explain in a minute. Maybe what you said to your neighbor, co-worker, or friend was something you would never have thought offensive. But it appears that it was. So you're now inclined to say, "*If* I said something offensive, I'm sorry." Nope, as I mentioned before using the word if is not the best way to go. Take responsibility for the offense and clearly state, "I'm sorry I offended you. Please forgive me." Or just, "I'm sorry I said something offensive," and move on. This will keep things smooth, and it will preserve the positive impression others have of you.

Here are some common examples that show how much more meaningful your apology is when you resist adding the word "if."

Not Proper	Proper
"I'm sorry **if** I took your seat."	"I'm sorry I took your seat."
"I'm sorry **if** I was talking too loud."	"I'm sorry I was talking too loud."
"I'm sorry **if** I hurt your feelings."	"I'm very* sorry I hurt your feelings."
"I'm sorry **if** I was late."	"I'm very* sorry I was late."

Including the word "very" in each of the instances above and below makes the apology more personal.

At work: Everyone who has ever had a job or will have one should know how important it is to have rapport with co-workers and a good personal reputation in general. But sometimes, it's just a word here and/or a word there that can work against a person. So even in the world of work, say no to the word *if*.

Not Proper	**Proper**
"If I forgot to refill the copy machine with paper, I'm sorry."	"I'm sorry I forgot to refill the copy machine with paper."
"If I forgot to copy you on my last memo, I'm sorry."	"I'm very* sorry I forgot to copy you on my last memo."

The latest unspoken insult is when someone sends an e-mail or a text message, but does not get an answer. When someone sends you an e-mail or a text message, be polite and respond. Even a short reply will do.

"Perfect. This really helps."	"Great."
"Just what I need. Thanks."	"Got it."

But if you didn't respond

Not Proper	**Proper**
"I'm sorry **if** I didn't respond to to your latest message."	"I'm very* sorry I didn't respond to your latest message."

Or, in text language

"IMS if I didn't respond to your latest message."	"IMV*S I didn't respond to your latest message."

Initially, most people thought the Internet would set us free from the social confines and cultural rules we inherited: sending thank-you notes for gifts and parties we attended, postcards while on vacation and letters to relatives and friends. Another rule we all understood was to make our calls at convenient times for others, certainly not during the dinner hour, late in the evening or needless to say, in the middle of the night. But with electronic tools at hand, it became easy to zap out e-mails, text messages, and tweets anytime the mood seized us. Furthermore, we heard back from everyone—*immediately*. But now that the novelty has worn off, too often we wait—and wait for a reply. Don't let that happen. This is definitely a social rule that has not changed: Answer those e-mails and text messages promptly. The courtesy of a timely response affects how people perceive you. Don't leave an impression that marks you as rude or inconsiderate on those you know or have just met with whom you have interacted electronically. People may not say anything, but trust me, they're thinking about a poorly made impression.

Pitfall Number Four: The Super Negative Yes ... But!

How many times have you heard—or even said yourself—comments, such as the following?

"I really think you're a great guy, Marvin, **but** long term, I don't think our relationship is going to work out."

"Yes, it was a wonderful meal . . . **but** I think it might have been just a little too salty."

"Oh, it's a great outfit . . . **but** don't you think the tie is a bit too loud?"

The implied "yes"—or the actual use of it—sets up the listener to think this is going to be a positive statement. In reality, though, that doesn't happen. **But** is a negative word that can cause more harm than the user intended. *The reason:*

It negates anything that was said before. Try to avoid using **but** in instances similar to those illustrated here because, just as you would perceive such comments as contradictory and negative, so will those you are addressing.

Knowledge leads to power. I hope by now we can agree that you have acquired a lot of knowledge in the art of talking to people you had never met before. Some people say knowledge is power. Others say that knowledge is just information and only becomes power when you put it to use. This book is about acquiring the knowledge to *meet and have a conversation with anyone, anywhere, anytime*. Practice, practice, practice, and the knowledge you're acquiring will give you great power when you put it to use. Your feelings of shyness about meeting people *for the first time* will be converted to confidence. That's power.

Chapter 14

The Give and Take of Criticism

Human beings have basic psychological needs. Certainly self-esteem is one that ranks high for all of us. We need to be valued and treated with respect and to treat others in the same way. So, when we're on the receiving end of criticism, sometimes it hurts our feelings and can even make us feel demeaned.

The good news is that being able to handle criticism is a skill, and as is true with any skill, it is one you can learn and become good at. Yes, this will take practice on your part, but once you've mastered the skill, you'll find the pay-off is well worth the effort. *The key to handling critical remarks is learning to externalize them. Believe me, knowing how to do this will make your life better.*

The Truth Doesn't Always Have to Hurt

Probably the most important thing to keep in mind when others say you offended them in some way or they criticize you for something you did, is to *accept it as a basic truth* . . . however much at the moment you may disagree. Here's the important point. *It may not be your truth, but it is the truth for the party or person making the criticism.* So, when you are silently thinking about how to respond, *always remember* that those who refuse to make an apology when it is obviously called for are usually considered insensitive and ill-mannered.

The best action to resolve criticism: Do not argue or strive to defend yourself. Graciously apologize and/or accept the criticism.

"I'm sorry I hurt you." (You forgot you had made a lunch date with a friend.)

Or:

"Thank you for sharing your feelings with me about that." (The person criticized something you are wearing.)

Two Ways to Go

Occasionally, you may find to your surprise that you actually agree with the other party's comments. This doesn't mean they make you happy at the moment, but in the long run, they could be quite valuable. That's why often the best resolution is to take a deep breath, be appreciative, and say thanks for the information. If the criticism is constructive, think of it as how people feel after a serious session at the gym. If they don't ache a bit, they probably didn't work hard enough to make any real improvement to their health and body. Constructive criticism can also be painful, but, like a workout session at the gym, it, too, can be quite healthy. So, when criticism is *constructive*, don't hold back about acknowledging it:

"Thank you for telling me that."

"Thank you for pointing that out to me."

"Thanks! You just did me a big favor."

Of course, there likely will be many times when you absolutely don't agree with the criticism. In this case. You are dealing with *your truth* and it is important to acknowledge this to yourself. (Please, though, do it silently.)

"Okay, that's the way that person feels, but it is not the way I feel. That's how he thinks, but not how I think. To that person this is truth, but it isn't my truth—nevertheless, I'll be nice about it, civilized, and courteous."

Accepting criticism in this manner provides the formula for both parties to move past the incident without damage to either's ego or to the relationship they share. You can do this because you didn't take the criticism personally. In other words, you externalized it.

I'm not suggesting that criticism is ever easy to take. But learning how to accept and deflect even poorly rendered criticism through depersonalizing and externalizing it will make you a happier person. We all face those moments when someone comes along who has something unpleasant or even mean to say about us. Whenever possible, let it go, put it out of your mind, and your life will be the better for it.

Studies have shown that people who accept criticism well and easily and apologize when it is appropriate are viewed more favorably than people who can't or won't. In the eyes of others, being able to accept criticism and to apologize when appropriate are signs of self-esteem. It is not a bad quality to have and to be seen as having.

Make It Real

When accepting criticism or apologizing, be sure your body language and tone of voice are in sync with your words. Look sincere and speak in a respectful tone. Studies have repeatedly shown that when there is conflict between a nonverbal and verbal delivery of a message, people nearly always believe the nonverbal one. That's powerful information, so pay attention. If you scowl and sound annoyed while making an apology or accepting criticism, others are apt to see you as hypocritical, which is probably not how you want to be perceived.

Here's an example of how body language and tone of voice can change the meaning of words. Let's take as an example the common expression, *"That's brilliant."* If after hand-ing in a report at work your manager shakes your hand, smiles and clearly states, "That's brilliant," you know he really liked your report and at least at the moment thinks you are brilliant. On the other hand, say you are at a party and you accidentally spill a glass of red wine on the person standing next to you. This person leans forward, frowns, and in a sarcastic tone says, "That's brilliant." You know you definitely didn't do anything brilliant.

Another point to think about and to remember. Sometimes, when people criticize you, it often tells you more about them and their likes and dislikes than it does about you. Train your mind to think this way. It will get you headed down the path of being able to externalize criticism.

Giving Criticism

The flip side of taking criticism well is the ability to give it well. Criticizing in a constructive way can lead to personal improvement, while delivering it in a destructive manner can close the door to a relationship. Incidents that trigger criticism are generally loaded with emotion, especially for the offended party, and this makes the memory of them last longer in a person's mind than you could possibly imagine. Here's the cardinal rule to keep your criticism from being destructive: *Criticize the object or action, never the person*. This depersonalizes any criticism you make and makes it much easier for the other person to accept.

Instead of:

"You look lousy in that blouse. I don't like it"

Try this:

"That blouse doesn't do you justice. It doesn't bring out the best of you which is pretty great."

Or:

Instead of:

"You look like a bum for not shaving."

Try this:

"It would be so much better if you shaved before we went out. Then, you'll look like your great self."

Or:

Instead of:

"That was a terrible report you handed in last week."

Try this:

"Kenneth, can you go back and bring this report a little more up to speed. I know you can do it, and it will remind everyone why we agreed you are the right person to do your job."

Remember these—they will get you through the thorny briar patch of criticism:
- Don't let criticism dampen your day.
- Keep an open mind.
- Don't take criticism personally.
- Stay focused on the message.
- If the criticism is correct, make the necessary changes.
- If appropriate, say thank you or apologize.
- Ask some questions to clarify the criticism.
- Disconnect and refuse to internalize the criticism.
- Soften criticism of others by addressing the problem, not the person.

Chapter 15

Introverts and Extroverts
What You Should Know About Each Other

My intention in this chapter is to shed light on the differences that exist between introverts and extroverts. I'm hopeful this information will give you the freedom to totally enjoy being whichever one you are. And as an aside, to allow your opposites to be who they are without any judgment.

Many people readily interchange the pronunciation and spelling of introvert and extrovert. Some say *introvert* and others *intravert*. Or *extrovert* vs. *extravert*. Take your pick, as all are correct.

Carl Jung, the brilliant twentieth century Swiss psychologist, popularized the terms extraversion and introversion. (For those of you who didn't take Psych 101, Jung is pronounced Yoong.) The major difference between extroverts (extraverts) and introverts (intraverts) revolves around how these types prefer to use their time and inner energy. In general, extroverts have a high energy level, are outgoing, openly expressive, and enjoy interacting with lots of people, individually or in groups, on a daily basis. Introverts, on the other hand, are energized by being alone, with their focus directed inward toward their own perceptions and projects including an avocation, a hobby, or something from work. Introverts like to contemplate, reflect, ponder, and think. But although they may engage in fewer social interactions, introverts do socialize.

Let's make some comparisons, so you can easily see the differences between extroverts and introverts.

Extroverts

Being friendly, gregarious, and socializing with people in various activities is a natural and fun way of life for extroverts. In the earliest stage of meeting someone, extroverts are easy to get to know, as they are very open, upfront, and have no trouble spontaneously expressing their thoughts, ideas, opinions, and feelings. Extroverts enjoy conversations to hear what others think, so they can better express and share their own ideas. You could certainly run into more extroverts than introverts at community meetings, public demonstrations, and political groups. But please note, I said more—not all.

Extroverts tend to make decisions quickly and are eager to take action. Their enthusiasm often translates into a predilection to do lots of things at once. In all probability, the multi-taskers you know are extroverts.

Introverts

Introverts, on the other hand, have a personal preference for being by themselves. As the saying goes: *"They are least alone when they are alone."* Introverts like people. Let's not have any doubt about that. Although they tend to have smaller circles of friends than do extroverts, they do socialize, have friends, are married, date if single, go to the gym, and talk with people at work or in their neighborhood. But they need more time in between these activities to recharge. In short, it's not that introverts can't socialize or don't know how. It's just that they would rather do less of it than extroverts.

Introverts tend to focus on one thing at a time and prefer having some time to analyze a situation prior to making a decision. But if they have to, they will decide quickly.

While extroverts burn out being alone too much over the weekend, introverts burn out socializing and interacting with too many people over the weekend. As you can see, introverts and extroverts become energized through opposite approaches to their daily lives.

Studies indicate that the majority of people are extroverted. The others are either introverted or somewhere in between—ambiverted. (I'll explain that shortly.) If you're an extrovert, happily accept the probability that many introverts compare themselves to your socially outgoing way of life and use it as a standard to judge their own. Also, many young people see being extroverted as a goal for the way they want to be once they grow up and enter the adult world.

Why? Extroverts always seem to be friendly, outgoing, having a good time and, *at least from the outside looking in*, somehow finding a balance between their social life and work. They also appear to have high self-esteem, a positive, enthusiastic approach toward life, and are certainly representative of the outgoing culture America personifies around the world.

Consequently, introverts may sometimes fret and wonder to themselves why they aren't *out there* like the extroverts. But, on the other hand, extroverts sometimes wonder when their social calendar is brimming over if introverts have the right idea. *"It would be so nice to stay home this weekend instead of gallivanting around. But I can't."*

Life in Between . . . Ambiversion

Some of you may be wondering why it seems so difficult to choose which camp you find yourself in. If so, relax, there's a reason. *Ambiversion* is a term used to describe people whose personality traits and social inclinations fall more or less toward the middle of the scale, somewhere between extroverted and introverted.

Sociologist Kimball Young coined the word in 1927, no doubt based on the dictionary definition of *ambi*, a prefix that implies "both" or "both sides." Ambidextrous, for example, describes people equally at ease writing with their right or their left hand. *Ambiverts* are comfortable with and enjoy an active social life, but also cherish and diligently plan for their time alone. Depending on what's going on in their lives, they can gravitate to either side.

Don't judge yourself and don't judge others. As you read this chapter and think about your friends, co-workers, family members, and even yourself, remember that being introverted, extroverted, or ambiverted is not a choice. As the old quote goes, *"What nature plants, the environment grows."* A great deal of who we are and what we do in life starts and ends within the brain, which after all is what allows us to see, hear, feel, sense, touch, hate, and love.

Neuroscientists through the use of functional Magnetic Resonance Imaging (fMRI) are beginning to confirm what has long been assumed: Certain parts of the brain are structured differently in those who are extroverted and their opposites, those who are introverted. In short, many of us actually are hard-wired from birth with an overwhelming predilection toward being one or the other or somewhere in between. Consequently, trying to change extroverts or introverts into who they are not, would be like trying to train a Bengal tiger to become a vegetarian.

Major Differences that Come Naturally

The following examples describe some ways that extroverts and introverts live. As you will see, there is nothing wrong with either side. They simply are what they are—different. For example:

Extroverts prefer and tend to wear stylishly decorative and individualistic clothing. Introverts prefer and tend to wear more traditional played down clothing.

126

The vast majority of those who enter the world of politics are extroverts, while the majority of men and women who dedicate their life toward perfecting one art form or another are introverted. It isn't enough to want to paint, write a novel, sculpt, or compose a symphony. You also have to spend hours and hours involved in your obsession, and not mind the time alone.

The idea of spending a weekend fishing alone on a secluded lake is an activity that would inspire many introverts and horrify most extroverts.

Extroverts who often stay home feel like they're in a rut. Introverts who often stay home feel like they're in heaven.

For you students . . . If you're a student, it might be helpful to know that extroverts find it harder than introverts to allocate time for studying alone. The pull to be out and about socializing is strong. If you think you're an extrovert, now you'll know why there's always an inner struggle for your time. But remember, just as your introverted friends often force themselves to attend parties when they would rather not, you, too, can force yourself to spend more time alone studying.

For extroverts, words of encouragement and words of caution when meeting someone for the first time:

First, some encouragement. As I've discussed in previous chapters, open-ended questions are a useful and constructively helpful way to:

- Get to know someone
- Keep a conversation going
- Learn about new subjects from people you meet

Now, some caution. When meeting someone for the first time, my advice is to avoid open-ended questions that are too open-ended.

- "What's new and interesting in your life?"
- "What's your biggest passion in life?"
- "How's it going?"
- "What do you do for fun?"

Why? At least 30 percent of the people you meet in life are introverts. Many introverts are also shy. As an extrovert, you may find it difficult to imagine why someone who is either shy or introverted would find it hard to spontaneously answer such questions. But they probably will, and as a result you may find yourself closing the conversation you thought you were opening.

"What do you do for fun in your life?"

"Oh, not much."

End of conversation

Even though it is a built-in instinct for humans to instantly begin the process of making judgments and forming opinions about people they meet for the first time, figuring out if someone is an extrovert or an introvert generally takes more than a few seconds, even for a trained psychologist. That's why you should be careful with these kinds of open-ended questions.

Sally is the mayor of a large city in the Midwest. She is constantly busy during the day and into the evening hours attending community meetings, talking with members of the press, leading staff meetings and, having appointments with scores of people who seek her help or support for various community projects and issues. But when the day is done, she gladly meets and catches up with her friends. Although a bit tired, Sally is personally and emotionally satisfied with her life.

Her sister Monique, on the other hand, finds satisfaction and fulfillment staying home alone as often as she can, in order to pursue her passion for painting classical art. With the front door to her house shut, the windows closed, the TV, radio and Internet off, the phone on mute, and her cat peacefully asleep on a small rug in the corner of the room, Monique is enveloped in happiness and self-fulfillment.

Now who is to judge if either sister should change?

Chapter 16

For Digital Natives
Advice from a Digital Immigrant

Digital devices have changed everything so much and so quickly, it is hard for me to remember what life was like before we had them. Certainly, I'm in absolute envy of the way those of you who grew up with these electronic tools negotiate your way effortlessly through them. What a delight that technology makes it possible to:

- Contact and chat with friends in a second or two wherever you are, whenever you want.
- Research almost any subject in great detail while seated or walking about, whenever the mood strikes.
- Listen to the music you want, whenever you want without ever hearing a commercial.
- Find and make friends with people from all over the world even though possibly you will never actually meet.
- Know you can always find your way with a GPS to guide you.
- Chat, tweet, and surf your way throughout your day.

Having grown up in the changed world, you are able to accomplish all of this with gadgets small enough to fit in your pocket and without giving even a thought about how to do it. **I can't.** But as enviable as your skills are, there's also a down side to this new way of life as it involves personal interactions. It's important for digital natives to understand what they are and how to avoid them. And I'm glad to tell you, you absolutely can. **Let's get started.**

What sets you apart from other people? It's how you communicate and not just electronically! Face-to-face interpersonal communication skills have always mattered and they still do. A lesson you began to learn early in life is that the world pays attention and people judge. You may remember when you left kindergarten to start the first grade how the teacher returned a homework assignment or test to you with a mark in the upper right hand corner of the paper. Perhaps it was an A+ or A, B+ or B, C+ or C, and, heaven forbid, not worse than that. But whatever the grade was, it marked the time and place in history when you and the other children in the room officially learned—possibly for the first time—that *the world keeps score.* People are going to judge you on how well you learn, memorize facts, and pay attention to the subjects the teacher had been explaining.

Fast-forward now to entering the world of work. School with its many restrictions is over, but once again, whether you like it or not, think it's fair or not, people will now judge you on how well you communicate on a person-to-person basis. As a striking example of how important these in-person communication skills are, I'll tell you about an experience I had a few years ago.

I was part of a search team that pre-screened candidates for a prominent, internationally known law firm's annual "internship" project. As with any search, there were a few underlying requirements. The applicants had to come from the five top-ranked law schools in the United States and they must have graduated in the top 10 percent of their class.

Is this fair? Is it legal? Apparently so. I have no doubt that every one of you reading this story, after taking a deep breath and perhaps rolling your eyes in amazement, will conclude that *knowledge* had nothing to do with which candidates were hired. After all, these candidates were all *certifiably brilliant.*

The point is, when a company is interviewing candidates to fill a position, it isn't always knowledge that determines who ends up with the job offer. More often, it's how well the candidates relate *and build rapport* with those who interview them. In other words, it's the quality of their *interpersonal communication skills.* These are the same skills you must have to get a job and other important things you want in life. Study after study has shown that good interpersonal communication skills lead to social as well as career success. In short, if you have good communication skills, you'll get what you want more often. Take it as a basic eternal truth.

Picture this. You're hanging out with three close friends when, without explanation, one of them takes out a book and starts to read. You and your two other friends cease to exist as far as the one now reading his book is concerned. Transpose this scenario to having a conversation with adults and suddenly taking out your smart phone to scan the screen for a minute or two.

This is also behavior that is ill-mannered and insulting to those around you, and believe me, the adults are silently calling you out for it. Do yourself a favor and make it an inviolate rule: When you are in the presence of adults, including co-workers, *practice will power.* Keep the phone in your pocket and your reputation intact.

The Power of Listening

For those of you who will be or are in the job market, here's an important tip. Most people brush up on their interviewing skills by learning what to say and how to say it. An excellent idea. But listen up. Good listening skills are as important in a job interview as good speaking skills. Listening intently when interviewers speak demonstrates that you find what they're saying interesting.

To show you're paying close attention, literally sit on the edge of your chair, lean in toward the interviewer, make eye contact, and let those "mmm's," "ah ha's," "Thank you for telling me that" and "Yes, that's a good point to know" comments keep flowing. The conclusion: People hire people who they think are qualified for the job and also the person who they like and feel will fit into the work environment. *When competing for a job, there may be other candidates who can out talk you. But no one can out listen you if you put your mind to it.*

William Gladstone and Benjamin Disraeli

In the mid-nineteenth Century, Great Britain had two great men as Prime Ministers, back to back. William Gladstone was Prime Minister in 1886 and Benjamin Disraeli in 1887. While both were brilliant, Gladstone was known for his soaring oratory and Disraeli for his brilliance as an author *and as a good listener*. A society woman had the good fortune to lunch with each of the men at different times during the course of one week.

In a newspaper interview, a reporter asked what it was like to meet such gifted and brilliant men. "While I was with Mr. Gladstone," she said. "I thought I was with the smartest person in the whole world. But after having lunch with Mr. Disraeli, I thought I must be the smartest person in the whole world." (I guess he did listen well!)

There's absolutely no doubt in my mind that taking full advantage of the technologies created by the geniuses of the digital revolution is a must for most people. Smart phones, iPads and Blackberries, just for starters, are necessities for millions of us for our work and daily life. But these gadgets will never replace the need to perfect face-to-face interpersonal social skills.

A great deal of what is important to people in their lifetime, at work or elsewhere, requires interacting and communicating with other people. And you know at this point, I'm not talking about text messaging. You can't "instant message" your way through meeting potential in-laws, establishing friendly relationships with co-workers, welcoming new neighbors, socializing with guests at a friend's house, or meeting new people anywhere, anytime in America.

In Western societies and certainly in the United States, people judge our wit, integrity, sincerity, humanity, intelligence, and of course, our knowledge through our interpersonal face-to-face communication skills.

Of course, I'm not going to suggest that you leave your electronic devices at home—that would be as ridiculous as my great-great-grandfather urging my great-grandfather not to buy a car, but stick with the family horse and buggy instead. My great-grandfather bought the car anyway and became a safe driver.

The reason: He learned the *rules of the road*. Similarly, you can attach yourself to your current devices or whatever new ones come along in the future, but you also must learn the rules of the road when it comes to these devices and face-to-face communication. The stories are now legend about young people glancing repeatedly at their Smartphones during a job interview and then posting on Facebook in amazement that they didn't get the job offer. Need I say more?

Obviously, the decision about how much of your day and your life you want to spend interacting with your gadgets is up to you. But please keep in mind as you grab your phone to play a video game or send another text, these gadgets were created for your use. But which of you is really in control? You may own these gadgets, but in daily life, do they own you? Give it some thought. It may be time for you to take back control.

Social Skills Matter

Here is a second story I read some time ago, long before the thought of writing a book entered my head. I don't remember either source, but I do remember the stories. In a subtle but everlasting way, they had a profound effect on my thinking. I hope they will help you as well.

Arturo Toscanini 1867-1957

Arturo Toscanini is considered one of the most brilliant and acclaimed musicians ever. In addition to conducting at New York's Metropolitan Opera and LaScala in Milan, he conducted all over the world. However, for all his fame, his lifelong shyness prevented him from developing good social skills. A wealthy matron once called the famous conductor to ask what his fee would be to conduct at her garden party. Toscanini replied, "My fee is ten thousand dollars."

"That's outrageous," said the woman, and hung up. The next day, she called back, a slight dent in her ego, and said, "All right, I'll pay you ten thousand dollars, but you're not allowed to mingle with the guests."

"Why didn't you tell me that yesterday, madam?" Toscanini replied. "In that case, my fee is only five thousand dollars."

No matter what other qualities, traits, talents, and gifts you bring with you, social skills have always mattered and always will.

The Generation Gap Lives On

From practically the first moment of this country's history, people have been coming here to reinvent themselves. And it seems to hold true for those who are born here as well. Each new generation reinvents the distance between it and the one that came before, proving that the Generation Gap is alive and well. You may now be behind the gap—or perhaps you've moved into the front. Wherever you are, though, the gap doesn't change, only your position in it.

For those of you in the younger generation, even now you can see there is a generation behind you, babies in playpens and strollers. One day soon, these kids will no longer be babies, and one day, they will inevitably view you as you did your parents' generation—old-fashioned, out of touch, and mired in a "socially constricted" way of life. To every generation coming into its own, the past is, as social anthropologists like to say, *"A different country."*

I'm hoping that whatever generation you're in, you'll be tolerant of those who are older—and those who are younger. Members of the older generation mean well and speak from their hearts, offering what they've learned to be wisdom. But I have hopes that the people in the older generation will respect and accept the younger one's way of life as well. All generations need freedom to grow into who they are even though it will undoubtedly look and sound different from the previous generation.

But let us all remember whatever our generation, there are basic *rights and wrongs* that will always exist. Social customs change regularly, but moral values never do. It's the way life should always work no matter what generation you happen to be in.

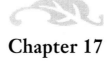

Chapter 17

Join the Crowd
Parties and Other Large Social Gatherings

Parties and other large social gatherings are usually planned around events that people want to celebrate and/or acknowledge. However, once there, instead of taking part, many invitees spend much of their time sitting back, silently observing the comings and goings and the hustle and bustle around them. They are aware of the fact that there are accepted rules of social interaction taking place, but they can't decipher what they are.

What kind of party person are you? Some people slink into parties, while others make grand entrances. After reading this chapter, you should be able to enter smoothly with composure and self-confidence because you will have learned the dynamics of large social gatherings and how to engage other attendees.

A Close-up Look

Let's put parties and various social functions under a microscope for a close-up look. Parties are fluid affairs. As we observe a party under a microscope, you'll see how groups of twos become groups of threes, how fours become two sets of two, sixes become threes, and so on. "Joining in" is going on everywhere, all the time. Imagine going to a party where people were locked into groups of two, three, or four, and not allowed to reconfigure except every half-hour! It would be ridiculous. You can see that a party or gathering then is a kaleidoscope of movement, and you can be a part of the action. The challenge is to have fun, while mingling both with people you know and those you don't.

Good Party Practices

Come early even if you intend to stay late. Some people, anxious about mingling, intentionally arrive late at parties. One unintended consequence of this strategy is that the late-comer potentially faces a scene of overwhelming activity and people who are already connected. Coming to a party early is a better plan of action because the host or hostess is usually free to introduce guests to one another as they arrive. At the very least, it will be easier for you to meet and greet people on your own as they enter. Then, you'll feel comfortably involved in the event as it develops because:

• You will have had a chance to meet several people before the party heats up.

• It's easier to blend into groups when you know at least one person.

• You will feel more of an insider if you've been there for a while. If you come late, you start as an outsider. Having a sense of belonging at a party, of being an insider, is a much better and more relaxed feeling.

Join In. It is perfectly appropriate at parties and other large social gatherings to introduce yourself to strangers. Let's say a co-worker invites you to her engagement party. As you enter, you notice a number of people who are standing or sitting by themselves. There are also a few sets of twos, threes, and fours. In the corner are five people huddled together. Which is the easiest group to join? Which is the hardest? Which would you avoid? Which would you gravitate to?

Here's a rule of thumb. When you see two people or two couples talking, there is a greater possibility the conversation is more personal than general. The introduction of a third or fifth person into the encounter could create an unwanted interruption. Consequently, it's usually easier to join an odd-numbered group. This isn't to say you can't break into groups of twos or fours, but odd-numbered groups are more approachable.

The most approachable of all, however, is probably someone standing alone. Maybe you've been that person, standing by yourself thinking, "Please send someone nice over to talk with me, so I don't have to stand here trying to look happy while feeling anything but."

When you approach a person standing alone at a party, a wedding, a business convention, or any other gathering, keep in mind that person may be alone because he or she lacks the skills you are now developing. If so, this person is likely to appreciate anything you say to start a conversation. As I discussed in Chapter 2, your ice breaker should include either a question or a declarative statement, or a combination of a question and a declarative statement.

• "This party sure is crowded. Irwin and Eileen know a lot of people."

• "This is a terrific electronics show. Did you see the new iPad display?"

• "Isn't Joan, the bride, beautiful? My name is Nick. I'm one of the groom's friends."

• "This is such a beautiful yard for a party. And the weather is perfect for it today, isn't it?"

• "Isn't it nice to see so many people come out for such a good cause? I'm glad I came. And the food isn't bad, either."

An important tip straight from my heart. Don't give the appearance that you're on the run when you approach people or they approach you. Be there for them. Stop, square off, face them, and don't look around the room. Encapsulate yourself. People usually interpret someone's not facing them while talking as having a lack of interest, a nonverbal cue that communicates not being fully committed to the encounter. That may not be how you feel, but others can take it that way. A good way to be sure you're showing real interest is a technique the most sophisticated conversationalists use: *point your heart toward the heart of the per-*

son you're talking with. (Think of it as having a "heart-to-heart" conversation.)

When talking with two or three people, turn to face whoever is speaking at the time. As the conversation shifts, turn toward the new speaker. Like all nonverbal communication, this will become a natural, unconscious movement once you've practiced it a few times.

Assimilating into a large group. People who regularly attend parties or large gatherings are accustomed to moving from one conversational group to another as they mingle or make the rounds. In fact, many feel obligated to do so. Clusters of people continually form and disperse, so you shouldn't feel slighted when someone spends only a short time with you at a networking event, party, wedding, or other large gathering. After all, when you're talking with a group and someone joins in or leaves, you seldom give it a second thought. Right?

The process of becoming part of a group begins by casually placing yourself at its outer perimeter and observing and listening for a minute or two. If the subject being discussed doesn't interest you, you can simply walk away. People do it all the time and no one consciously notices. Partygoers refer to this as "keying in" or "getting a sense" of the conversation. If you like what you hear, stay and engage. Here's how:

A helping hand. Say you're standing just outside a group when a friendly person makes eye contact with you. If you respond with a head nod, an eyebrow flash, and a brief smile, you are in. It's that simple. (You'll remember from reading Chapter 9 that an eyebrow flash is a single up and down movement of the eyebrows that implies recognition.)

To further integrate yourself into the group, call on one of the conversational cues you now have in your arsenal for meeting anyone, anywhere, anytime. Remember, whether you're alone or in a group, conversational cues are socially accepted verbal and/or nonverbal signals that tell people you're interested in making contact with them. For example, you might respond to a remark someone just made by casually saying to the person standing next to you:

"Yes, I think he's right."

"That was a funny line."

"I had a similar experience just the other day."

Sometimes, even a simple "acknowledgment" is all that is needed.

"Right"	"You're kidding"
"Wow"	"Oh, really"
"I agree"	"That's interesting"

Find the odd person out. Another tactic when approaching a large cluster of people is to look for the "odd person" out. When five or six people are in a conversational huddle, someone is likely to be on the edge, partially disconnected from the group, involved, but not committed. Approach the group and stand idly by the odd person out. Often he or she will step back or to the side to make room for you. Then, at the appropriate time, simply pop in with a declarative statement or a question.

"She made an interesting point."

"This is a fascinating topic."

"By the way, my name is . . ."

A mutual connection. If you're at a party, wedding, charity function, or gathering of any kind, everyone in attendance has a connection to the event. The cultural rules of engagement, not only allow people to be open and friendly to those they haven't yet met, but they also encourage them to do so. If you were hosting such a function, wouldn't you want it that way?

Hosting and identifiers. At any gathering, whether you're a host or a guest, when you introduce someone you know to someone you just met, do what good hosts do and add an "identifier." An identifier is a detail about a person.

Party: "David, I'd like to introduce you to Marcy. Marcy and I just met. She knows Margarite (the host) through work. Marcy, David is an old friend of mine."

Wedding: "Abby, this is Neal. Neal is Michael's uncle. Neal, Abby is my first cousin."

Office Party: "Annie, this is Nita. Nita is in the accounting department. Nita, Annie and I work together in sales."

Tennis Club: "Yvonne, this is Barbara. We just met. She joined the club recently. And Barbara, watch Yvonne's serve if you play against her. It's deadly."

Hi! My name is . . . I'm often asked, "When is the best time to introduce myself to a person I've just met?" The answer is the sooner the better. We all know the longer you wait, the more awkward it becomes. Sometimes, you meet someone and believe the encounter won't last long, so why exchange names? But then the conversation continues and you feel uncomfortable about this lapse of not introducing yourself. Chances are the other person feels the same way and is also wondering why he didn't introduce himself.

Don't expect the other person to take the initiative. Although he may realize he should introduce himself, he may not know how. Many people don't have the conversational skills or the awareness that you're developing of how to engage people. If introductions are needed, assume it probably will be up to you. When introducing yourself, it is the time to play host and to add your own identifiers. Be friendly. Maintain eye contact, smile warmly, and say:

Birthday, Anniversary, Engagement Party: "By the way, my name is Mack. I'm Julian's golfing buddy."

Office Party: "By the way, my name is Ruth and I work in sales."

Antique Show: "By the way, my name is Ann. I'm a collector and have been for years."

Resort Cocktail Party for New Arrivals: "By the way, my name is Lon. I flew in from New York. This is my first time here."

Did you notice how all of the suggested ice breakers above:
- Incorporated an environmental prop?
- Were casual comments using plain, simple English?

These identifiers help the person you just met become a better getting-to-know-you conversationalist by giving him or her, in just a few words, conversational fillers to expand on.

"Oh yes, I know Julian loves golf. I'm his next door neighbor."

"I'm in accounting. I've seen you around the office a few times and wondered what you did at the company."

"I'm also a veteran collector. Been at it for years. How did you get started?"

"Oh, you're from New York! I'm from Chicago and it's my first time here, too."

In many places where people meet, an identifier is not obvious. If this is the situation, all you need to say is:

"Oh, by the way, my name is Justin."

"Oh, by the way, my name is Justin. What's yours?"

"Oh, by the way, my name is Justin Brown. What's yours?"

Any of the above is appropriate. Use the wording that seems most comfortable for you.

The good news is that it's never too late to introduce yourself even if some time has gone by since you started to chat. Monitor your own feelings the next time the person you're talking with belatedly takes the initiative and says, "Oh, by the way, my name is Justin. What's your name?" Note how natural this seems and the confidence the person you're talking with must have to initiate the introduction so late in the conversation. Next time, that self-composed person could be you.

Guilt, Guilt, Guilt. For our purpose, guilt is an emotion coming from the realization we have ignored or violated a standard social expectation. "If we once met, you'll remember me and know who I am forever more." Just as we expect people to remember us, others carry that same expectation. Say you bump into someone you were introduced to in the recent past. As your mind races to recall the person's name, you smile and attempt to cover up your memory lapse by saying, "It's so good to meet you again." But adding to your anxiety, the other person greets you by saying, "Hi, Marvin, funny bumping into you here."

Don't panic, and don't hesitate for even a nanosecond. Maintain eye contact, offer an embarrassed smile, put your hand on your chest, and say,

"I am so embarrassed. Of course, I remember you. But I'm terrible with names. Please tell me yours again."

Or:

"This always happens to me. Names, why are they so hard to remember? And it's worse since you remembered mine. Please, tell me your name again."

I'm not aware of any scientific polling data on the number of people who regularly forget other people's names, but from my observations, I'd say it's in excess of 80 percent.

The best spots. Great fishermen know where the fish usually bite, golfers know the best golf courses, and gourmets know the best restaurants. At parties, two of the best "meeting-people places" are at the bar and around the hors d'oeuvre table. People seem freer to talk at those two locations. *The Reason:* These areas provide the most conversational props. Although most people don't know what conversational props are, they unconsciously use them all the time.

147

"Have you tried the shrimp yet?"

"I wonder what's in that delicious-looking dish."

"And to think I started a diet today!"

Of course, hanging out at the bar or the hors d'oeuvre table takes discipline and willpower, lest you drink too much or overeat. But if you can deal with the props in moderation, head in that direction. Note: If you're drinking, hold the glass or bottle in your left hand. Then, if you shake hands with someone, your right hand won't be wet and clammy.

It's not just you. Let's say you're supposed to meet a friend at a party. You arrive on time, but your friend is late. You enter a large crowded room with about a hundred guests who are talking, laughing, smiling, eating, and drinking. People don't always wait for Halloween to wear a mask to a party. Many of the people in the room are as uncomfortable as you are, but their masks say otherwise. Ninety percent would never consider starting a conversation with someone they don't know because they don't know how.

So, the shyness you feel mingling at a party with strangers is far more common than you realize. Unless you're already an extrovert, this chapter won't convert you into "the life of the party." However, with time and practice, it should enable you to relax and enjoy parties the way most of the guests are only pretending to!

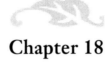

Chapter 18

Singles Meeting Other Singles

In every country, there are idiomatic expressions or figures of speech that are commonly understood. For example, I would bet everyone in the United States knows what these mean:
- Apple of my eye—someone much adored
- Bite the bullet—decide to do something important
- Let the cat out of the bag—give away a secret
- Am I talking to a brick wall?—referring to a stubborn person
- Well heeled—someone with money

Here is one we also often hear and, like the others, we understand. **"I would like to meet someone."** We know that doesn't mean meeting just anyone—this is shorthand for "I would like to meet someone special I could really like and who could maybe be in my life for a long time."

Needless to say, it assumes that the "someone" you have in mind will feel the same way. He or she would be attracted to you, feel you're special, and think maybe the two of you could make a go of it for a long-term relationship. Well, my friends, as obvious as it may sound, in order to "meet someone," you must first meet them. In other words, you can't meet the "right person" without meeting people.

And by the way, if you're a part of the older generation, don't think for a moment that age makes it impossible to meet the "right person." A colleague of mine pointed out the difference in how people today age. "When I was a kid, lots of 70-year-olds walked around with a cane. Today, they're walking around with tennis rackets," he told me. Every year several hundred people over the age of 65 run the New York Marathon! Everyone is younger today than we used to be, and, besides, who said you don't want a romantic relationship, whatever your age.

It's a process. I'm not sure anyone has figured out a way to create spontaneous attraction—it's something that just happens. As human beings, most of us can't really determine in advance the person we will fall for. What we can do, though, is select the people we approach to meet. Most single people, wherever they live, have a deep desire to meet Mr. or Ms. Right. The trap that many of them fall into, however, is focusing on the goal—"If I could only meet someone tonight!" With that attitude, they overlook the process that would take them to the goal. It's not enough to want to meet someone—you have to be willing to go through the process to get there. And that is what this chapter is all about.

Online dating has become part of our culture and that's great. But there is no way meeting online can totally replace the potentially magical moment when you see or meet someone who intrigues you in a way you can't explain, even to yourself. Often it happens in a time and place you least expect. It isn't the Fourth of July, but sparks are flying. How then do you go about approaching this person to let her or him know you're interested without coming on in a way that could squelch the result?

Words that Might Change Your Life

The following strategy is one of the best I've ever heard for single adults to deal with their fear and be able to meet another single person for "social purposes." Social purposes, of course, means dating, the process we use in our culture to explore the potential you have with another person to create a long-term relationship. Please take these words to heart— they represent what is truly a remarkable strategy for meeting another single person for *"social purposes."*

When you see a single person, someone of the opposite sex* you're attracted to and think you would like to meet, use the environment you're both in, find an environmental prop, and make up your mind to approach this person and proceed to interact as if he or she isn't a single person of the opposite sex that you're attracted to and interested in meeting.

***A disclaimer**. Although I make references to opposite-sex attractions and interactions, in no way do I mean to exclude anyone in this discussion. My intention is only to imply another person who catches your eye for a possible intimate, long-term, romantic relationship. The strategies I am describing here hold true for everyone—gay, lesbian, bi-sexual, or heterosexual.

Put the magic words to work. Say you find yourself standing next to someone you sense you're attracted to. Would it be so difficult for you to say:

• At a museum. "Abstract art is so interesting, isn't it?"

• At a workshop during a break. "I've taken classes with this instructor before. I think she's very good."

• At a party. "I'm a friend of Megan. We were neighbors when she lived in San Francisco. How about you?"

• At the beach. "This sure is a great day to be at the beach, isn't it?"

"All the good ones are taken." So why are so many people either getting engaged or married every single day in America? Some expressions should be banished forever.

Advice for Men

Every day in this country, literally thousands and thousands of men see women they think are attractive and would like to meet, yet never go over to them. Why? What stops them? Men put a great deal of pressure on themselves by believing that when they approach a woman in any public area for social purposes, they must start the conversation with a pickup line. "What can I say that she'll find witty, charming, funny, sophisticated, and gallant?" But as they struggle to come up with a witty, charming, funny *pickup line* the clock is ticking. In the end, most men can't think of what to say, so the moment passes and with it the opportunity.

What kind of line . . .
- "What a cute dog. Does he/she have a telephone number?"
- "I never believed in love at first sight until I just saw you."
- "I think I'm in heaven because you look like an angel."
- "Could you please call 911? My heart stopped beating just by looking at you."

Men, not only are the lines above not meant to be memorized—they represent the kind of lines you should always avoid. I doubt there are many woman who would like any of these or find them even remotely funny.

You may be relieved to learn that you can meet a woman anywhere, anytime without resorting to a pickup line. Keep in mind as I explained previously, when you first engage a woman you think you would like to meet, you aren't doing it as a pickup, but as a *casual encounter*. Present yourself in a relaxed fashion with a slight smile on your face or in your voice.

This attitude will indicate that you're a man who has confidence in himself—and women like that. Because few men approach a woman out of the blue, any man who does must be confident. Even on first meeting, women often base their attraction to a man on the way they respond emotionally to him—that is why a confident presentation is so important.

When you look around for your environmental prop to start the conversation, be sure you don't choose one that is too personal, such as commenting on a woman's figure. The exception (and there always seems to be one) is only when it's personally not personal.

For example, a comment about an individual ability such as "You are really a terrific dancer," or tennis player or swimmer is personal without being offensive in any way. What would turn it into being offensive would be if you added something like this—"I can see that dancing [or tennis or swimming] works for you. You have a terrific body."

Let's review for a moment. If you see a woman who has caught your eye, go over to her, allowing for a distance of about three feet between you, so that you don't crowd her. (If she's already standing within speaking distance, you don't even have to walk those horrifying steps to make the approach.) Then, find a safe environmental prop, and speak.

• A break from a lecture or workshop (seeing a woman who looks as interesting to you as the subject you came to study)—"I'm enjoying this lecture/workshop so far. How about you?"

• At a museum (a woman you find more interesting to look at than the painting in front of you)—"Excuse me, I don't want to break your train of thought, but what do you think of that picture?"

• On an airplane (a woman whose presence raises your heart beat and sends your imagination flying)—"Gee, it looks like a full flight. Every seat seems to be taken."

• At the gym (standing next to a woman who wants to lose a few pounds that you think look great exactly where they are)—"It doesn't seem as crowded tonight as it usually is."

In all probability, the woman will not run away, but will stop to have a conversation with you, especially if it's one of those unexplainable magical moments when two people out of the world's seven billion cross paths and meet, or rather, they connect. Then, if after talking for a while, the chemistry seems right, you can convert the casual conversation into a more personal social one.

Believe me, if the woman is interested, she'll do her bit to move this forward—women are extremely clever about this. But if the chemistry isn't there or you suddenly notice a ring on her finger, you can disengage smoothly, casually and politely say goodbye without anyone's ego getting bruised. (See Chapter 8 if you need to refresh your techniques on saying goodbye.)

Starting a friendly conversation with someone who interests you, not only takes the pressure off you, it also takes the pressure off the woman you approach. Whether for safety or social reasons, human beings tend to experience a second or two of anxiety when someone they don't know comes over to start a conversation.

Unconsciously and instinctively they do an evaluation. What's going on here? Who is this person? Why does he want to talk to me? What will we talk about? A casual, low-key approach helps avoid startling a woman in this way and that is crucial.

Compare that for a moment to how you would feel if one day you're standing in a line at, say, the supermarket or the movies and, as you turn around, there's a woman staring at

155

you and in effect saying, "Hey, big boy! I'm looking to meet you. To pick you up." With a flirtatious smile, she asks, "Did anyone ever tell you, you have beautiful eyes?"

Her message is obvious and, of course, there aren't many women who would ever come on this way. If that were to happen, though, your immediate response would likely be to think, "Whoa . . . hold on. I might be interested, but it would be nice to have a minute or two to figure this out." You can easily see why pickup lines and an aggressive approach, whether a man's or as in this case a woman's, just don't work.

Advice for Women

It is my observation that women spend a lot of time, thought, and energy making themselves attractive before they venture out into the world. To the delight of men everywhere, congratulations, you're successful in your endeavors. *But this does not make you approachable.* Let me explain.

Most women when in public places seem to have perfected an attitude that I call a first cousin to what the brilliant sociologist Irving Goffman termed *"civil inattention."* Goffman used this to describe the way people barely acknowledge one another in such places as elevators or waiting in line.

Women on the other hand, when in the presence of a man in an elevator or when walking down the street, or in a mall, or anywhere else, do so in a state of *"social inattention."* Not even for a second do they make eye contact. They walk either looking distantly straight ahead or keeping their focus on an electronic device. The message they impart—which probably contradicts their wishes—is, *"I'm not looking at you, you don't exist, and it would be best if you don't talk to me."*

The common belief is that women are always on the lookout for a relationship. But guess what? The reality is that *so are a lot of men.* Why then put up barriers when, with no extra effort, you can pave the way for men to meet you? For example, say you're at a singles event with a group of friends—can't you take an occasional break from laughing and chatting with the pack to walk around by yourself?

It's hard enough for guys to approach women, why make it harder by hanging out with a group? If you want to meet one of the men at an event, you'll improve your chances by making it possible for him to approach you. Or, here is an earth-shaking idea. *You can approach the man.* But remember, not as someone you're attracted to, just as another human being.

For example: *"It sure is crowded here tonight, isn't it?"* Trite, corny, unsophisticated. Yes! Absolutely. And it's also a line that would stop any man in his tracks if said by a woman in an aerobics class, concert, art gallery, wine-tasting event, coffee shop, gym, sporting event, party, wedding, charity function, resort hotel . . . *anywhere!* At any age, it's cool for a woman to show her confidence in being able to talk first to a man in a public place. A woman who does is rare and rarity has value.

A Few Important Asides

• Whenever and wherever you approach a man or a man approaches you, whether it's in a retail store, waiting in line, or while getting your morning coffee, *stop, make eye contact, smile, and speak.* Believe me, nothing about what you're wearing is more attractive to a man than your smile and making eye contact.

157

• If a man is interested, a few minutes of chat will give him time to muster the courage to ask for your phone number or e-mail address or to suggest a time to meet again. Or you can take the lead to offer a method of connection with which you're comfortable.

"I have to go, but perhaps we'll meet again. I would enjoy that."

"I have to go, but hopefully we'll bump into each other again. I would like to finish this conversation."

"I would certainly be interested in seeing that show (movie, ball game, art show) with you. It could be fun to go together."

• Long ago, mothers would tell their daughters, "It takes a smart girl to play dumb." As I said, that was long ago. Today, many men feel there's nothing more attractive than a confident, competent, and smart woman.

• Men don't just like femininity, they love femininity and women who enjoy being a woman. And why? Because that helps guys feel like a man.

• "Can you help?" Dated though it sounds, men are eager to step forward when a woman needs help. They love to be the hero of the moment. If you need help, don't be reluctant to speak up. Even if it's just a jar you're having trouble opening. *Ask him to do it for you!* I know you may be thinking I'm just kidding around, but I'm not. When a man is needed to help a woman, it gives him good feelings about himself and makes him proud to be the man of the moment.

For Men and Women—Fear Lives in Us All

The most serious obstacle that stands in the way of meeting other people, especially when it's someone of potential romantic interest, is fear of rejection. In truth, this fear is a normal human reaction and the reality is it never goes completely away. Even the most successful, popular, and self-confident people—I'm talking about men and women—hate the idea of personal rejection.

Since the fear won't go away, your best strategy is to accept that you're experiencing a fleeting, unpleasant feeling, one that won't ruin your life and in all likelihood you'll forget in a few days' time, or probably even a few hours. As a friend of mine once wisely pointed out, "If you're single, why let ten seconds of potential embarrassment lead to a long-lasting regret? *If you see someone you're interested in, make the approach. Don't let a fear of rejection determine your future.*"

When you see a single person, someone of the opposite sex you're attracted to and think you would like to meet, use the environment you are both in, find an environmental prop, and make up your mind that you'll approach this person, and proceed to interact as if he or she isn't a single person of the opposite sex that you're attracted to and interested in meeting.

Keep Anxiety at Bay. In your mind, embrace the magic words above before you approach someone who has caught your eye. It will help take your ego out of the experience, and that will keep the fear of rejection from being uppermost in your thoughts. Also, keep in mind that you don't have to actually feel confident to appear as if you are. You may never lose a bit of nervousness whenever you put this technique to use, but that is no reason the other person will see this is how you feel. Most people have feelings of shyness when first speaking to strangers and if there seems to be a mutual attraction, remember that the fear of rejection is not gender-specific. Now it works both ways.

Now a Few Words About Flirting

I know some people think the notion of flirting is silly or "beneath" them. That is definitely a mistake. Flirting has existed historically in every culture in the world. You might not recognize the signs of flirting in places with customs very different from ours, but trust me, on some level, it's going on wherever you are. Flirting is a time-honored tradition for people to get to know another person who is or may become a romantic interest.

In most places and events, certain rules of social restraint are in practice as I have discussed in this chapter. However, there are situations where some standard rules of social behavior and interactions are temporarily put on hold and replaced by more uninhibited ones. This is called *cultural remission*.

At any event that involves cultural remission, people are expected to check some of their usual social inhibitions at the door along with their coat. For example, let's say you have gone to a singles event where people go to meet possible romantic partners and where alcohol is served. You can be sure that the laws of cultural remission will be in effect.

Singles who take part in any event whether at a bar, club, or private party that caters to singles and serves alcohol are not there to have intellectual conversations about world events. Attendees understand that the goal is to meet *someone*.

Consequently, the idea of flirtatiously showing someone you're interested in him or her can and should start sooner rather than later, in fact, almost immediately. After all, that's why everyone is there.

The exception to our rule of cultural remission has to do when the event is a wine tasting. Even though wine is, of course, alcohol, social behavior concerning wine drinking is more subtle than when other forms of alcohol are served. Treat a wine tasting as you would a lecture, fund-raising event, or other more formal social gathering. Put what you have learned in this chapter to work, meet people who interest you, and then, when it's clear something is happening here, let the flirting begin.

What can happen while standing in line. I was standing in a bakery in my New York City neighborhood recently when a beautiful Asian-American woman came into the store and stood next to me waiting to be served. **What happened?**

The bakers were busy in the back when suddenly a heavenly aroma filled the air. Using the environment around me, I said, "Wow, what a great smell! It makes you hungry, doesn't it?" She smiled back, lighting up the whole room, and said, "It is a great smell and you're right. Now I am hungry."

My intention was neighborly only, but I was struck by how within five square blocks of where we stood, there had to be **at least** fifty single men who would have gladly taken my place. I also wondered how many of them would have shied away from using the environment around them to start a conversation with her because of her beauty and would have ended up walking out of the store with only a blueberry muffin and not even her name.

It's not just men who are intimidated into silence—women, too, miss these kinds of opportunities on a daily basis. Of course, most encounters come to an end after a pleasant comment or two, but so what? They still give you a chance to be charming and engage a stranger, making your city or town seem a bit smaller.

On the other hand, maybe the conversation wouldn't end there—maybe this brief encounter would be *the* one that leads to a lifetime of shared conversations. You'll never know if you never try.

Concluding Words

Time and time again in my life, I've seen the wisdom in the old expression: "Each ending brings the possibility of a new beginning." This seems particularly apt as we come to the end of this book. My hope for you is that what you learned in it does indeed represent a new beginning. But you alone can make this decision and take that first step.

In effect, a new beginning starts with the simple act of looking for a conversational prop with which to start a conversation with another human being and then enjoying the pleasure of making a connection, however brief it might be. Having developed the skill of meeting and communicating with people who minutes ago were strangers doesn't in any way change the essence of who you are. Better than that, it allows others to share in what that essence is.

How long will it take? Unlike mastering most skills, be they golf, ballroom dancing, playing guitar, self-defense, bridge, and so many others, mastering the skill of meeting people doesn't take long to perfect. You'll be encouraged to continue and to polish your newfound ability by the friendliness, surprise, and even relief others will extend to you for being the one to speak first.

"Every person born into this world represents something new, something that never existed before, something original and unique." —Martin Buber, 1878-1965

Some things don't change and Martin Buber's long-ago observation is as true today as when he said it. As a result, every encounter you engage in with *anyone, anywhere, anytime* will be at the very least slightly different from any others. Soon, though, you'll see that all of them share an underlying structure.

As you have now learned, every conversation starts with either a question, a declarative statement, or a combination of both, which leads you onto a two-way conversational path. It might take you to a super highway, a city street, a scenic mountain road, or a quiet country lane. The scenery is different, but the *rules of the road* will always be the same.

As you put these rules into play, I wish you good luck—and a lifetime filled with good conversations.

About the Author

Marvin Brown began his career in sales as a Financial Planner. While doing so, he participated in what was then the largest mutual fund sale in the history of the Financial Services industry. But he soon came to realize that he had an innate understanding of the social skills planners need to reach their true potential. He decided to transfer into sales management where he became the National Sales Manager of the Dreyfus Corporation, at that time the second largest mutual fund group in America. Marvin was also the Founder and first President of the New York City chapter of the Financial Planning Association.

Marvin personally trained thousands of men and women at national and regional conferences in the art of selling themselves when presenting clients with financial planning products and services. Today at workshops around the country, he teaches a wide variety of people the social and conversational skills that enable them to more fully engage in and enjoy their life. Marvin is the owner of Contact Strategies, LLC in New York City where he also resides. This is his first book.

To Order This Book

To order additional copies of this book,
please go to:
www.contactstrategies.us

This book may also be ordered from 30,000
wholesalers, retailers, and booksellers in
the U. S., and in Canada and over
100 countries globally.

To contact Marvin Brown for an interview
or a speaking engagement,
please send an e-mail to:
marvin@contactstrategies.net

CPSIA information can be obtained at www.ICGtesting.com
Printed in the USA
BVOW010040030713

324900BV00007B/191/P